LEADERSHIP COMPETENCIES in ORGANIZATIONS

Crown Publishing Company, LLC.

LEADERSHIP COMPETENCIES in ORGANIZATIONS

ARE YOU A RULER, MANAGER, OR LEADER?

What makes you one?

Crown Publishing Company, LLC.

LEADERSHIP COMPETENCIES in ORGANIZATIONS

ARE YOU A RULER, MANAGER, OR LEADER?

What makes you one?

A. OLU OYINLADE, PhD.

Crown Publishing Company, LLC.
P.O. Box 540821, Omaha, Nebraska 68154, USA.
https://crownpublishingcompany.com/

ISBN: 978-1-967372-01-0 [Hardcover]
ISBN: 978-1-967372-00-3 [Paperback]
ISBN: 978-1-967372-02-7 [E-Book/Digital Book]
ISBN: 978-1-967372-04-1 [Audio]
Library of Congress Catalog Card Number: 2025935708

Cover Design (with AI assist): A. Olu Oyinlade
Interior Design: A. Olu Oyinlade
Chief Editor: A. Olu Oyinlade
Associate Editor: Lisa Quals

Crown Publishing Company, LLC.

CONTENTS

DEDICATION.. xi

ACKNOWLEDGEMENTS xii

INTENDED AUDIENCE xvi

PREFACE... xvii

SECTION 1: THE CONFLATION PROBLEM............... xx

CHAPTER 1: INTRODUCTION 21

CONFLATION PROBLEM 22

    Raison D'être.. 26

CONTENT LAYOUT... 30

SECTION 2: DIMENSIONS OF HEADING A GROUP . 33

CHAPTER 2: ARE YOU A RULER, MANAGER, OR LEADER?... 34

DIFFERENTIATING AMONG CONCEPTS................... 35

RELATED CONCEPTS IN HEADSHIP 47

    What is Management? 55

What is Leadership?...57

CHAPTER 3: UNDERSTANDING MANAGEMENT 61

ESSENTIALS OF MANAGEMENT FUNCTIONS AND
PRINCIPLES.. 62

FUNCTIONS OF MANAGEMENT 63

Planning and Forecasting 65

Organizing.. 66

Commanding.. 68

Staffing and Coordinating................................... 71

Controlling 73

PRINCIPLES OF MANAGEMENT...............................74

The Principle of Division of Work..........................75

The Principle of Authority and Responsibility 79

(Fayol, [1917] 2013)...79

The Principle of Discipline.............................. 80

The Principle of Unity of Command 83

The Principle of Unity of Direction.................... 84

The Principle of Subordination of Individual Interest 86

The Principle of Remuneration........................... 88

The Principle of Centralization 89

The Principle of the Scalar Chain........................91

The Principle of Order.. 94

The Principle of Equity... 96

The Principle of Stability of Tenure 99

The Principle of Initiative 101

The Principle of Esprit De Corps 102

CHAPTER 4: BEHAVIORAL CHARACTERISTICS OF MANAGEMENT 105

IDEAL-TYPE MANAGEMENT CHARACTERISTICS. 106

Goal Orientation.. 108

Manager-Subordinate Relations....................... 112

Bureaucratic Authority: Authorized Power 114

Obedient Compliance by Subordinates............. 117

Management Techniques 119

Bureaucratic Activities and Status 132

Doing Things Right 134

Maintenance of the Zone of Indifference.......... 136

CHAPTER 5: UNDERSTANDING LEADERSHIP 141

LEADERSHIP IS INFLUENCE.................................. 142

LEADERSHIP COMPETENCIES.............................. 145

Informal Status 145

Goal Attainment.. 152

Influence Through Endorsed Power 155

Followership 161

Doing the Right Thing 172

Courage 184

Voluntary Extraordinary Performance 194

Human Relations Techniques 198

Vision Orientation 200

 Provision of Protection 207

 Good Political Skills 212

CHAPTER 6: OVERVIEW AND TAKEAWAYS 215

REVISITING HEADSHIP 216

The Management Factor 216

The Leadership Factor 219

CITED WORKS 225

INDEX 243

ABOUT THE AUTHOR 251

DEDICATION

I find it most befitting to dedicate this book to all the students who have taken my organizational studies classes, both undergraduate and graduate, over the past three and a half decades. I have had the privilege to educate you and be educated by you on all matters relating to complex organizational structures, employee performance, and leadership behavior. A special dedication to this book also goes to the students who honored me with the opportunity to mentor them here and there at one time or another. While such students are too many to list in this dedication, in particular among them are Mackenzie Reuss, Zachary Christo, Katie Hayne, Anna Jensen, David Finch, Carrie Lacy, Lara Tewksbury, Tom Shirazi, Branden Mitchell, Deanne Barrett, Jill Annis, and Bryan Holzhey. This book is dedicated to the opportunity to explore knowledge with all of you. And very importantly, I also dedicate this book to my daughter, Bisi, who is a budding middle school mathematics and science teacher. As the head of her classroom, she will benefit from many of the ideas contained in this book about the different ways to head a group.

ACKNOWLEDGMENTS

Writing a book as a solo author, publishing it, and bringing it to the market is a major ordeal. The daunting work involved at several junctures, from the conception of a book idea to writing the book and getting it published, while simultaneously managing the several competing demands of a professional career and personal life, often hinders potential authors from writing their books. But when one is surrounded by a network of positive and encouraging people, one is able to find a way to successfully manage all competing demands and accomplish one's writing objectives. Such is my experience. I am fortunate to have a network of incredibly positive and encouraging friends who have supported me in various ways from when I first conceived the idea of a leadership book through all the writing and publishing stages. These friends include Mr. Lawrence Diggs, with whom I first discussed the idea of this book about seven years ago. As a published author himself, "Mr. Vinnegar Man," as Lawrence is nicknamed for his work with Vinegar, his Vinegar book, and his Vinegar Museum, did not hesitate to encourage me to write this book. Every time I had the opportunity to discuss my teaching, research, or consulting activities with him, the Vinegar

Man would always remind me of the importance of writing my leadership book. In addition to his encouragement to write this book, he also shared many valuable ideas with me about possible publishing options. Without any doubt, his counsel and encouragement contributed to my motivation to write this book.

My good friend, Ms. Sherry Helmke, was also invaluable in her support for my work and ideas for several years. On many occasions, she generously listened to my ideas and gave me good advice on possible ways to accomplish my different professional goals. I value her deliberations with me about how to get this book into the hands of those who will most appreciate it. I sincerely appreciate Sherry's patience in listening and suggesting various ideas to me over the years. She is a gem in my corner.

Like the Vinegar Man and Sherry, I also had some deliberations about this book with my long-term friend, Laura Vosika, who is also the author of many books and the proprietor of a book publishing company. Laura was positive about this book. She shared knowledge with me about the nuances of book publishing, competing ideas in book publishing, and how to avoid publishing mistakes.

And, very importantly, she willingly gave me good guidance in the publishing process.

It is essential that I also recognize my good friend, Scott Powers, for the invaluable stories of workplace behaviors and manager-employee relations that he has shared with me over the several years of our friendship. His stories educated me and enriched my perspectives on leadership behaviors that could enhance the transformation of managers into leaders. Some of the experiential stories that he shared with me appeared in this book with some modifications.

My friends, Dr. Christopher Achua and Dr. Gerry Cox, also matter greatly in bringing this book to light. Both Chris and Gerry are also book authors and career academics. As a leadership textbook author, Chris was very supportive of this book and gave me strong encouragement to get it done. But when I was having difficulty getting started, I wrote an email to Gerry in January of 2021 and told him about my desire to write a leadership book and how I was having difficulty getting started. He wrote back with a simple message that I should just start writing. He said:

"Writing [a book] is just sitting down and doing it. With my work on the Habitat for Humanity house, I am often tired, but I still try to write for at least an hour before I give it up for the day. A little each day is a good way to get started. Good luck with your books. Be well. Gerry."

With those few words from Gerry, I began writing this book and its successor the following day and continued writing until I completed both. This is the first of the two books. The second book, titled *"Leadership Behaviors for Managers,"* will soon be available for purchase on Amazon, bookstores, and many other outlets. The book discusses behaviors that build the followership that transforms a manager into a leader. It is a book that I also highly recommend for anyone who wishes to become a leader to others in an organization.

Thank you, Lawrence, Sherry, Laura, Scott, Chris, and Gerry. A special thank you also goes to Emma Eitzmann, my co-worker, whose excitement for this book was very encouraging. She enjoyed hearing my progress on the book, and she eagerly waited for its release. I appreciate her enthusiastic support very much.

It is time for more managers to become leaders. I have great faith that this book will be an invaluable tool and a starting point for many managers on their journey to becoming leaders.

INTENDED AUDIENCE

This book is written purposely for anyone who wishes to become a leader. It is specially written for individuals who have others reporting to them. Such individuals include high-level corporate and business executives, directors, managers, and supervisors worldwide. Administrators in government, education, not-for-profit organizations, and business owners are equally targeted as the audience for this book. Others who will benefit from this book include corporate trainers, human resources professionals, and other organizational development specialists who assist managers in developing leadership competencies. In addition, because this book is based on academic, scientific foundational knowledge in a textbook style, it can be used as a textbook by university and college educators who prepare students for organizational leadership across industries.

PREFACE

Are you a ruler, manager, or leader? This question is the subtitle of this book for a reason. It is intended to challenge you, the reader, to reflect on your dominant way of relating to others in the workplace. It can be argued with good logic that everyone who heads a unit, whether a division, department, or workgroup, will at some point relate to others based on the characteristics of each of these three relational approaches. However, as a general pattern, the unit head will most likely exhibit the attributes of one of the relational patterns more dominantly than the others. That dominant pattern will define the unit head, and it will have consequences on the performance of the workers who report to that person. It will also have other outcomes, such as job satisfaction, motivation, and organizational commitment.

Without a doubt, the three headship relational approaches differ from one another, but the most generally preferred pattern, as many studies and authors have concluded, is leadership. This is evident in the countless leadership books that have been published to encourage managers to become leaders. Leadership is a highly attractive topic for business writers and academic researchers due to its significant value to organizations. Leadership brings much more to an organization than management. While management is an essential, crucial, and unavoidable part of any organization, the contributions of leadership can be argued to significantly expand employee productivity beyond what is possible through management alone. Hence, for any organization seeking maximum effectiveness and efficiency, as well as employee commitment, having leaders is essential to achieving these outcomes.

Unfortunately, despite the numerous books and research articles on leadership, these resources generally define the concept based on each author's conceptualization. Hence, the idea lacks a unified definition. In addition, these books and articles also fail to consistently distinguish between management and leadership and, in the process, equate them. Any manager who wishes to become a leader will not gain much knowledge about leadership competencies from those books when the concepts are used interchangeably.

If one is to become a leader, the first thing to learn is the different ways by which work units can be supervised, and that is the focus of this book. In this book, I examine the methods by which an individual can become the head of a unit within an organization. The book explains and discusses the main approaches to heading a group: the authoritarian ruler, the manager, and the leader. By reading this book, you, the reader, will gain much knowledge about these different approaches. You will gain valuable knowledge about what it means to rule, manage, or lead those who report to you.

The qualities that define each headship status are fully explained so that you will acquire knowledge about the virtues of each status and strive to gain desirable headship competencies, especially in leadership. While leadership is typically the preferred option for heading a group, you will also gain appreciable knowledge about the place of rulership and the importance of managers and management for organizational success. Although leadership is most desirable, rulership and management have their merits in organizational success. This is why all three relational styles must be well understood, and it is also why I invite you to read this book. Happy Reading.

A. Olu Oyinlade, PhD.
Business Organizational Sociologist
Professor and Leadership Development Consultant
https://crownbusinessconsulting.com/

SECTION 1

THE CONFLATION PROBLEM

CHAPTER 1
INTRODUCTION
Conflation of Concepts

Too Much Misunderstanding of
Concepts. Let's Get Them Right.

CONFLATION PROBLEM

This book has been on my mind to write for many years. It is a book that I contemplated for several years, but I delayed writing it due to a lack of time caused by several competing projects. Due to the importance of the content of this book, I did not want to dilute my concentration on writing it with other projects. Hence, the delay was necessitated. The book is definitely overdue, and now, it is finally here! It is informed by a rich knowledge base spanning 38 years of academic scholarship as a university professor in complex organizations, as well as my experience as a business consultant. The wait proved to be valuable. During the years of waiting, I deepened my knowledge of organizational leadership by gaining additional critical perspectives on the topic through my readings, research, teaching, workshops, conferences, and consulting. My accumulated knowledge and critical perspectives in organizational leadership over the years have added strength to the content of this book. This sets it apart from many leadership books, as I explain in the following paragraphs, and as the reader will discover upon completing the entire book.

One might ask why a book on leadership is overdue. Are there not enough books on leadership already? Is the internet not brimming with leadership books? And is there not a plethora of textbooks and training manuals on leadership in the market already? While the answer to these questions may appear to be affirmative, a careful review of most books, whether trade books, professional books, training manuals, or even textbooks, will reveal to a discerning reader an inconsistency in explaining and analyzing leadership.

The inconsistency is primarily a result of the conflation of concepts. The two concepts, management and leadership, are too often conflated. Many people, including managers and high-level executives, frequently misunderstand and regularly conflate these concepts. Unfortunately, so do most books, magazine articles, and scientific reports. These literature outlets typically offer little or no consistency in the meaning and application of these concepts. While it is common for many books to accurately highlight the differences between management and leadership in one chapter, the remaining sections of the same books often overlook those distinctions and misuse the concepts by conflating management with leadership. It is disappointing that, despite their assertions of the distinctions between the two concepts, most authors frequently describe management as leadership. They fail to be consistent in their conceptual, theoretical, and empirical discussions of leadership. This is especially surprising when one considers the credentials and caliber of many of the people who write books on leadership. Many of the authors possess extensive management experience, academic research, and teaching experience, so one would expect them to write about leadership without conflating it with management.

I must confess to being equally guilty of the conflation phenomenon in most of my earlier leadership studies. My realization that I was conflating the concepts occurred during a discussion of leadership with a graduate student some years ago. The student was interested in my leadership research at the time. In the middle of my explanation of key factors in my research, she asked why I was using the term leadership instead of management. She said she could not differentiate between management and leadership in my research and asked me to clarify for her why my research was on leadership rather than management. Despite my confident knowledge of the two concepts, I still made the conflation mistake, which I was lucky to realize through the confusion and queries of a good graduate student. This is how easy it is to make the conflation mistake.

The conflation mistake is so widespread that I describe it as a *commonly accepted standard error* (CASE) in leadership studies. However, we should not accept CASE regardless of how widespread it is and irrespective of the caliber of people who make it. This is especially important because of its implications for leadership development. For example, if both concepts are used interchangeably as synonyms, leadership development becomes management development and vice versa. By equating the two concepts, the value, advantage, or benefit of leadership over management is lost or compromised at the very least, and leadership development becomes redundant or completely nullified at worst. Notable authors, who ought to know better, publish research articles and books, including best-selling ones, that flagrantly conflate management with leadership. When they do so, what chances do students of leadership and practicing managers have in correctly distinguishing these concepts and accurately analyzing their positions as managers or leaders? Students and managers learn CASE rather than leadership. For current and future managers who may aspire to become leaders, the knowledge of management vis-à-vis leadership is not just beneficial but crucial. Without a clear understanding of leadership, they may find themselves perpetually exhibiting managerial actions due to a lack of proper education on the subject of leadership.

Raison D'être

Perhaps the raison d'être of this book is becoming apparent to the reader at this point. Raison d'être is a French term that means *reason for existence*. The reason for writing this book is to give a thorough discussion of leadership without conflating it with management. This is intended to provide a much-needed understanding of what leadership is and what it is not without any confusion. To this end, the chapters in the second section of this book will thoroughly discuss the concept of headship and distinguish between management and leadership in separate chapters. While this book is on leadership, two brief chapters are devoted to an understanding of management, primarily in its ideal-type, as outlined in the classic work of Henri Fayol (1841-1925), for comparison and contrast with leadership.

If a manager is to become a leader, it is essential to know what it means to be a leader compared to being a manager so as to have a clear understanding of the destination of one's intended transformation. In consistently separating management from leadership and not equating the two concepts, this book is a critical departure from the tradition to which the reader is most likely accustomed. While this book may be wholeheartedly welcomed and seen as long-awaited by many readers, it may equally be a mental challenge and disruptor for those who have accepted the tradition of conflating management with leadership. I hope that such readers will learn to unfreeze themselves from any previous misconceptions of leadership and allow themselves to absorb accurately consistent knowledge of the concept.

WE ALREADY HAVE GOOD MANAGERS. WHAT WE NEED NOW ARE LEADERS.

As I will discuss later in this book, with a citation from Tom Peters and Nancy Austin (1985), what US corporations need now are leaders rather than managers. American corporations are replete with good managers.

This is evident in the productivity of US businesses and corporations, which yielded a 2021 gross domestic product (GDP) of approximately USD 23 trillion, the highest in the world, accounting for roughly 24 percent of total global GDP (World Bank Data, 2021). However, this does not invalidate the cry for leaders over managers as indicated by studies such as Lowe et al. (1996) and Aragon-Correa et al. (2007), among others, which have shown a direct link between leadership and higher employee performance. Through vision-setting and the ability to influence followers to self-actualize, leaders are capable of achieving higher employee productivity, motivation, job satisfaction, and organizational commitment than managers.

Studies have "suggested that leaders manage to motivate employees to be competitive through charisma, inspiration, intellectual stimulation, or individual consideration" (Vasilescu, 2019, p. 48). If, despite their high productivity, US corporations still prefer leaders over managers, the demand for leaders can also be expected to be high in corporations around the world. The need for leadership over management appears to be especially critical as organizations seek success in navigating through domestic and global competitions, as well as adapting to rapidly changing performance technology and consumer preferences. So, simply put, regardless of how good managers might be, leaders are still preferred and in high demand. If this is true, the big question then becomes what qualities managers should attain to make the transition to become leaders. This is the main focus of this book.

If leaders are in high demand, it is a big error to tell managers that they are leaders because of their job positions and roles. This is to assume leadership in error, and it is an unfortunate CASE in leadership books and what has been described in many books as leadership theories. With a careful understanding of leadership, one will recognize that leadership is not a bureaucratic position. Rather, it is an informal social status earned from others. Unlike the Traits Theory of leadership, which assumes that leaders are people with special human qualities or unique habits, aptitudes, and abilities (Steers et al., 1996), this book is written from the more accurate reality and intellectual understanding that leadership is earned and bestowed rather than endowed by special natural abilities. It is also important to point out that this book is not about feel-good sentiments. It is not about becoming a leader by just being a nice person. It is about understanding specific technical qualities of leadership that managers should aspire to attain if they are to convert their subordinates into followers.

CONTENT LAYOUT

This book is written to provide knowledge for leadership development rather than to teach basic concepts and theories of leadership. It is written to provide practical knowledge for leader-aspiring managers on what qualities to develop to become leaders for those who report to them. In this regard, the core of this book is on leadership competencies development.

Based on the goal of this book, the best way to get maximum value from reading it is to study it purposely to gain leadership competencies. It is best to read the book in chronological order by section. To this effect, the content of this book is organized into two sections. The first section is the introductory unit, which comprises this chapter (Chapter One). The second section introduces the reader to basic concepts of headship in the five chapters that form the core of the book. The second unit begins with Chapter Two, which presents the reader with the concept of headship and its three major variants:

rulership, management, and leadership. The chapter also discusses the misuse of the concept of leadership and how it is commonly used as a CASE.

The third and fourth chapters discuss management. The functions, principles, and characteristics of management are discussed in the two chapters. Since the book is designed to guide current and future managers in their development of leadership competencies, it provides a good understanding of management characteristics as the beginning point of their leadership transformational process. It is also designed to give managers a brief refresher on the functions and principles of management.

The fifth chapter is devoted to a thorough understanding of leadership characteristics and how they differ from management. This chapter is crucial for understanding the leadership qualities or competencies that managers need to attain to become leaders. The chapter is also important for understanding why management and leadership are distinct forms of headship and why they should not be used interchangeably or assumed to be unitary. Lastly, the sixth chapter gives the reader a brief summary, overview, concluding remarks, and takeaways from the book. The chapter briefly connects all the dots of knowledge in the book with a stress on the importance of the value of managerial transition to leadership.

Since the five chapters in Section Two are intended for learning the characteristics of management and leadership, as well as learning to correctly distinguish the two concepts, the focus of the section is to build knowledge about different forms of headship and to give managers standard leadership qualities to attain. The chapters in this book provide sufficient in-depth descriptions of management and leadership to inform a manager of the characteristics of both concepts and the ideal leadership competencies to acquire. Lastly, Wherever the pronouns he and she and their equivalent conjugations are used generically to refer to non-specific persons, such as a manager or leader, the reader is at liberty to substitute a pronoun for a preferred one.

SECTION 2

DIMENSIONS OF HEADING A GROUP

CHAPTER 2

ARE YOU A RULER, MANAGER, OR LEADER?

Who are you to those who report to you? Do you rule, manage, or lead them?

DIFFERENTIATING AMONG CONCEPTS

Are you a ruler, a manager, or a leader? It is befitting to start this chapter with the subtitle of this book. It was probably the subtitle that piqued your curiosity and led you to want to read what the book contains. You probably felt compelled to read this book because you wear the hat of a supervisor, a manager, a corporate trainer, an executive, an administrator, or a Human Resource Officer. You are likely a student of management, public administration, organizational sociology, Industrial-organizational psychology, or other areas of organizational science. It is also possible that you are an educator, a consultant, or an organizational development specialist. And, of course, you may also be someone who loves to read and finds the topic of this book enticing. If you wear any of these hats, the chances are high that some people currently report to you at work. You may also be coaching others on how to be a good manager or how to become a leader. Chances are also high that you are curious about your own behavioral characteristics regarding how you relate to those who report to you.

Have you ever stopped to ask yourself whether you were ruling, managing, or leading the people who report to you in your organization? If you answer that you rule over your people because you dictate their actions, you have labeled yourself as a ruler. If you see yourself as managing your people because your relational behaviors fit what you believe are characteristics of management, then you have described yourself as a manager. Moreover, if you equate your relational behaviors to what you consider to be leading rather than ruling or managing, you have labeled yourself as a leader.

Regardless of how you may label yourself, it is essential to ask further questions of yourself. Such questions may include: Do ruling, management, and leadership mean the same thing to you, or do you believe they are different concepts and behaviors? If they are different, what behavioral characteristics comprise each of them? What are the specific supervisory behaviors you regularly practice that make you qualify yourself as a ruler, manager, or leader? Do you automatically qualify yourself as a ruler, manager, or leader mainly because you occupy a position of authority, high responsibility, and one that others are required to respect and obey? Do you believe being in charge or being the head of a unit simultaneously makes you a ruler, manager, and leader? If you believe you are a ruler or a manager, do you know who you are ruling or managing, respectively? If you believe you are a leader, do you know who you are leading? And, finally, what would you rather be: a ruler, a manager, or a leader? Why the one you prefer, and why not the other two? Answering these questions, and perhaps others too, will help you gain a better understanding of your supervisory or relational behaviors vis-à-vis those who report to you. Your answers will help you to recognize who you are and what you can become to those who report to you.

In 1979, Nigeria, my country of birth and where I lived through the end of 1979, had a government change from a military administration to a civilian one. This new civilian administration was dubbed the Second Republic by the Nigerian people. The dubbing reflected the second time democratically elected politicians had governed the country since it became independent from Great Britain in 1960. Between 1960 and 1966, the country had a democratic government, which was toppled in a military coup d'état and ushered in a series of military administrations until 1979, when the country returned to civilian rule in a new democratic government dubbed the Second Republic.

The second democratic republic in Nigeria encouraged the formation and active participation of multiple political parties. Five parties contested for the presidency, the national assembly, and state legislative seats (Metz, 1991). In one particular state, Ondo State, among its 66 legislative seats, 65 were occupied by members of one party, the Unity Party of Nigeria (UPN). The last seat was occupied by a member of another party, the National Party of Nigeria—NPN (African Elections Data Base, 1979; Ondo State House of Assembly, 1979-1983). According to house rules, the lone NPN assemblyman became the minority leader in the house.

One day, according to an anecdotal story, the supposed minority leader in that state assembly spoke to the house and complained about being treated poorly by the house members from the dominant party. He demanded to be treated much better and to be respected as the House Minority Leader. When he finished speaking, a member of the majority party (UPN) in the house rose to speak and asked if the honorable NPN member, who had demanded respect as the minority leader, would agree to answer a question. The question was, if the honorable representative were the minority leader, could he please point to whom he was leading? The questioner continued and said that if the honorable minority member was the only member of his party in the house, and if he wished to be recognized and respected as the minority leader, he must first show whom he was leading that qualified him as a leader.

Obviously, in a political arena, the party with the largest number of seats is recognized as the majority, and the head of that party is called the majority leader. Similarly, the parties with fewer seats are termed minority parties, with their heads designated as minority leaders in multi-party systems. These situations appear to suggest that a leader has followers. But what about the situation in which only one member of the house was a minority? Could a lone member from the minority party be correct in claiming to be the minority leader despite not having any other minority members in the house? Was this assembly member a leader? Who was he leading? Himself? Is being a leader the appropriate term for describing a person who is not in a group relationship?

We can also probe further about the positions of the majority and minority leaders in situations where there are multiple members of their parties in the house. Is the term, leader, truly appropriate in describing the status of the head of a party? When the terms leader and leadership are used, are they used correctly, or have we gotten used to the misuse of these terms such that their meanings become one of assumed knowledge, where we believe that once we use the terms, others automatically know what the terms mean? Alternatively, perhaps, the assumption is that these terms conjure different images in people's minds, and whatever image a person has is expected to appropriately guide the person's reactions to the terms.

When you pay attention to the use of the terms leading, leadership, and leader, you will notice people tend to automatically respond to them from their own interpretations of what these terms suggest to them rather than what the terms accurately mean. The likelihood is high that you, the reader of this book, also respond to the concepts of leader and leadership mostly from your own assumed meaning and personal interpretations of the concepts rather than their accurate meanings. By now, you are probably wondering about the correct meanings of these concepts. You are probably asking the question:

What constitutes leadership, and what makes a person a leader? One of the goals of this book is to explain these concepts in the most academically and intellectually accurate ways, starting with this chapter.

Leadership Misnomers

To understand leadership, it is important to clarify some misnomers about the concept. Here, I use misnomers to represent a misleading idea or a misleading meaning of an idea. Consider the following situation to understand a major misnomer about leadership. An army captain has been assigned the duty of commanding officer of his unit. If he identifies himself as the head of the unit, he will be correct and justified in claiming to be the head or the officer in charge. If a superior officer, a colonel, visits the captain's unit, it is most likely, given military lingo, that she would ask who is in charge of the unit. It is, however, also likely that she may ask who the unit leader is, and the captain may respond by signaling that he is the leader. But, is the captain the unit leader or just the unit head? If he is the leader, who is he leading? Is "leader" a correct term for the captain's status? How about you, the reader of this book? How would you answer these questions? Are you a leader? If you answer yes, who do you lead? What makes you a leader? What makes you think you are leading who you think you are leading?

According to Max Weber (1864-1920), the German philosopher, historian, and economist, the misnomer with the terms leadership and leader is that these terms are erroneously used to describe what sociology refers to as rational-legal positions of authority (Weber, 1947). Rational-legal positions can be defined simply as bureaucratic positions of authority within an organizational structure. These are positions that we occupy as members of groups and organizations. Everyone who is hired into an organization is given a job title and a place within the hierarchy of the organizational structure. The position that a person occupies within an organizational structure is a rational-legal status (or position). Consistent with the descriptions of rational-legal authority by Max Weber (1947), sociologist Robert Merton had earlier explained that every organizational member is assigned to a bureaucratic position that carries a job title to discharge the responsibilities of the position (Merton, 1936). An organizational position is rational and legal. It is designed as a legitimate part of an organizational structure that is backed by organizational power to effectively and efficiently contribute to organizational goal accomplishment. The position may be a unit head, unit chairperson, supervisor, manager, corporate chair, president, or chief executive officer. The office holders of these offices have supervisory or management responsibilities, but we often erroneously refer to them as leaders, and so do they of themselves. To call them leaders is a gross misnomer, and so it is for them to identify themselves as leaders. The president is only a president, and a manager is only a manager. These rational-legal titles do not mean leader or leadership. Unfortunately, this conflation of position with leadership is widespread and highly detrimental to leadership. As I mentioned in Chapter One, the conflation is so pervasive that practically every book and academic article on leadership is guilty of it. Even when leadership books and scholarly articles give accurate definitions of leadership and contrast their definitions with those of management, before long, in the same literature, the authors begin to conflate and equate leadership with management.

When we equate management with leadership, we undermine the meaning of leadership at the very least, and at the worst, we make leadership development almost impossible. It means that once a person occupies a supervisory position, the person is automatically a leader; therefore, all an organization needs to do to make anyone a leader is a promotion to the supervisory ranks. This conception is seriously detrimental to leadership development. The recognition that the occupation of a management position is not an automatic conferral of leadership is why boards of directors of business organizations have asserted that what we need in organizations is leadership instead of management (Halloran & Benton, 1987). This was also a remark by popular business consultants and authors Tom Peters and Nancy Austin, who decried that American businesses needed more leaders than managers (Peters & Austin, 1985). These assertions signal a message to corporate officers that, regardless of the loftiness, power, and prestige of their titles, they are still mainly managers. Without a doubt, no one (at least a sane one) would say corporate boards of directors are not surrounded by managers at the highest levels of organizations. So, it is safe to say that when comments are made that American corporations need leaders, not more managers, such comments point attention to the need for a different set of skills than management skills for guiding American corporations.

American boards of directors, as well as Tom Peters and Nancy Austin, are not the only people who have claimed that American organizations need leaders rather than managers. Several academic and professional writings on leadership have made similar comments. The call for leadership over management and administration is prevalent in both scholarly and non-scholarly reports on all forms of organizations across organizational fields and industries. A very telling example can be found in a 2016 article titled "Schools Need Leaders - Not Managers: It's Time for a Paradigm Shift" in the *Journal of Leadership Education* (Stein, 2016, pp. 21-30). The author, Dr. Les Stein, at Northeastern University, bolstered the need for leaders over managers, and in his case, in the education field. He indicated in his article that he was operating on a major premise that for American schools to be globally competitive, they must be led rather than managed (Stein, 2016).

If both business corporations and academic organizations, alike, need leaders rather than managers, anyone with a curious mind must ask what makes leadership so different and superior to management. And, given that some American corporations are among the most successful organizations in the world with managers at their helm, what is it that leaders bring to the table more than the managers who have already made many American corporations highly successful? The same question can be extended to American schools that have produced many great students who have become corporate executives, school principals, district superintendents, university presidents, governors, and much more. What is it that makes leadership superior to management, such that managers are numerous while leaders are scarce?

It is appropriate at this time to begin to unveil the meaning of the concept of leadership. But, because it is a concept that can be easily misunderstood and conflated with related concepts, it is best to first discuss those related concepts as foundational knowledge before delving into leadership itself. This approach will induce a better and more precise understanding of the leadership concept, as well as make the comparison of concepts easier for a deeper understanding of leadership.

RELATED CONCEPTS IN HEADSHIP

When we are members of an organization or a group, we automatically occupy positions within the structure of the organization or group. An elaborate discussion of organizational structure is outside the scope of this book, but for the current purpose, it is sufficient to indicate that occupying a position is an inherent nature of organizational or group membership. One of the positions one may occupy in an organization or any of its units is that of headship (being the head). That is, one may occupy the position of the head of the entire organization or any of its units or sub-units. The head of an organization may be the position of Chairman, Chairwoman, President, Superintendent, or Chief Executive Officer (CEO). Other positions one may occupy as a unit or sub-unit head may include Executive Vice President, Vice President, Assistant Vice President, Chief Operating Officer, Senior Manager, Manager, Department Chair, Dean, Director, Principal, Supervisor, Group Captain, and many more. As mentioned earlier, all these are positions that people occupy to discharge specific duties, typically involving the coordination of the activities of others for goal accomplishment. This means that being the head (or headship) is the generic term for all the numerous titles that describe offices that are charged with the responsibilities of coordinating the activities of others within a group or an organization. When a person occupies the position of the head of an organization or any of its smaller units, there are three main methods or types of behaviors the person may use to coordinate the labor of others within the organization or unit. They are ruling (or rulership), management, and leadership. Below is a brief definition and description of each of these forms of headship. Ruling is fully addressed in this chapter, but much more about management and leadership will be discussed in later chapters.

What is Ruling?

When the head of a workgroup, a department, a division, or an entire organization uses ruling as a preferred style of coordinating the work of others, this makes the head a ruler. The ruler turns organizational authority embedded in the headship position into raw power or absolute authority to dictate the activities of others in the organization or unit (Farh & Cheng, 2000). Other concepts that accurately capture rulership are dictatorship, authoritarianism, and totalitarianism. These concepts demonstrate the use of power by the ruler as well as explain some of the salient traits of rulership. These three concepts are often used as synonyms in literature (Chiang et al., 2000); hence, no distinction is made here about any nuanced differences they may have. What is essential in this discussion is that these concepts demonstrate how the ruler is fully in control of all aspects of organizational life and how the ruled workers, as subjects, must be overseen with an iron fist and regularly coerced into submission to the ruler out of fear of punishment. This is akin to asking "how high" when asked to jump because of the absolute authority of the ruler.

Absolute Authority. This can be described as an unrestricted, organizationally authorized power that a ruler uses to demand unquestionable obedience from workers (Farh et al., 2006; Pellegrini & Scandura, 200). It indicates that the ruler can use power without organizational or group restrictions. The person controls all decision-making power and suppresses the ability and opportunity of workers to express their ideas (Yun et al., 2005). He often dominates the decision-making process and determines work procedures and regulations based solely on his ideas (Purwanto et al., 2020). This is done by centralizing decision-making power and excluding workers from making suggestions or any contributions to decisions by preventing them from stating their opinions (Yun et al., 2005). By doing so, he is able to constrict the autonomy and self-determination of workers through the strict use of impersonal procedures and rules (Li et al., 2019).

The ruler, as an autocrat, may even use power beyond the limits of office without repercussions. He can suspend existing organizational policies that may restrict his position's authority, and he may replace them with policies that give him unlimited unilateral power. When this happens, he is either above the law or he becomes the law. The ruler dictates the activities of subjects. This includes the dictation of goals and methods of goal attainment. Rewards and punishments are also dictated and enforced with extreme use of authority. The ruler turns others, the ruled, in the organization (or, more specifically, those who report to him) into subjects who are governed through coercion and fear. This is a major distinguishing characteristic of rulership. Ruling significantly emphasizes the inducement of fear in the ruled.

Some Dysfunctions of Rulership. The negative side of rulership makes it unappealing and inappropriate in many organizational conditions. As indicated by Chiang et al. (2020), rulership is detrimental to the emotional well-being of workers because it suppresses it (Yao et al., 2022). By treating workers as subjects, the ruler is able to use organizational power to demand absolute obedience (de Hoogh et al., 2015) as workers are forced to achieve highly demanding objectives and mechanically follow rules (Li et al., 2018; Karakitapoglu-Aygün et al., 2021). Invariably, rulership creates enough relational dysfunction between the ruler and the ruled workers that results in attrition or intent of attrition from an organization, as it destroys employees' desire to commit to an organization (Schaubroeck et al., 2017; Koveshnikov et al., 2022). In addition, because it creates dissatisfaction with the organization, rulership discourages employees' creativity (Guo et al., 2018), hinders work performance (Chan et al., 2013), and discourages willingness to participate in organizational activities beyond required job engagements (Zhang & Xie, 2017; Wu et al., 2012a; Wu et al., 2012b). While the ruler, as an authoritarian, has been associated with traits such as high self-confidence (Li et al. 2019) and readiness to take all blame for any negative consequences of his decisions, he is also likely to usurp all credit for everything that went well under his command (Ridgeway, 1983; White & Lippitt, 1953).

Some Positive Outcomes of Rulership.

Based on the dysfunctional consequences of rulership, the first inclination is to automatically condemn it as an improper and unacceptable form of headship. However, each method of headship has value in the right circumstance, as expressed in the wisdom of the contingency theory of management (Yum et al., 2006).

Rulership produces some positive consequences under the right circumstances that are worth recognizing. For instance, rulership may be benign in cases when the ruler combines the absolute control of authority with benevolent concerns for workers' needs (Farh & Cheng, 2000). He selflessly looks after his workers and always has their best interests at heart (Farh & Cheng, 2000). In this case, the benign ruler makes decisions in the best interests of his subjects, even when he is feared. This example may be found in athletic coaches and military generals whose decisions are based on extreme power, which is used benevolently as necessary to benefit their athletes or soldiers, respectively. Authoritarian benevolence has been found in research to positively improve relative perspectives of job processes (Meng et al., 2022) and job performance (Hou & Peng, 2019). The authoritarianism of rulership has also been associated with the best form of headship when an organization is in disorder or chaotic conditions (Ridgeway, 1983; White & Lippitt, 1953) that often include goal and task uncertainties, role ambiguities, and conflicts among workers. Given that rulers have been credited for providing "clear directions and expectations regarding compliance with instructions" (Sanchez-Manzanares et al., 2020, p. 840), a ruler can use authoritarianism to single-handedly determine goals, tasks, appropriate task structures, and devise action plans without wasting time. He will order people to execute the different aspects of his plans and, in doing so, achieve organizational order and high employee performance in a relatively short period. The efficiency in his decision will save the organization from losing resources and even dying.

Using authoritarianism, the ruler has also been established as very effective in organizational conditions in which rewards are low, unit size is large, and the cost of failure will be devastating to a unit or even the entire organization (Rahmani et al., 2018). In these conditions, the ruler is able to use autocratic power to cut through any red tape and issue orders that force unit members to achieve all required goals to ensure unit or organizational success. This action may occur irrespective of workers' feelings, attitudes, or needs. This approach can also be witnessed when the ruler uses an authoritative command to stop interpersonal conflicts among workers. Unfortunately, such a command does not resolve disputes since the manager does not investigate the sources of disputes and apply proper corrective structural measures to solve them (Gibson et al., 2012). In time, these problems eventually erupt again. However, when the instructions of a ruler are backed by extreme power, the ruler can achieve great results from workers by force or coercion. He can set very high standards and coerce workers to obtain them by threat or actual infliction of punishment (Wang et al., 2013; Lee et al., 2019).

Perhaps authoritarianism works so well in negative work conditions because it is consistent with high-task and low-relationship decision-making characteristics that are most effective in reorganizing and regaining balance in conditions of workplace disorganization (Lussier & Achua, 2003). Interestingly, the authoritarian ruler is also successful in workgroup situations in which members cooperate and minimally contest for power (de Hoogh et al., 2015) as well as highly participate in the work process (Sagie, 1996). These conclusions from various studies support Fred Fiedler's contingency theory of leadership effectiveness, which states that the authoritarian management style can be highly effective at both extremes of social order –full stability and full chaos– in organizations (Fiedler, 1964, 1972). Also, in terms of the effectiveness of communication, the autocratic approach of the ruler means his instructions are backed with extreme power, which compels workers to comply and, hence, makes authoritarian communication effective and efficient (Karakitapoglu-Aygün et al., 2021).

What is Management?

Unlike ruling, management describes the use of position to effectively and efficiently allocate organizational resources, make good judgment in the prudent use of the labor of subordinates, and preside over organizational functions (Gardner, 2000). Essentially, the manager is the unit head who uses assigned bureaucratic power, that is, the authority of the office occupied, to determine who gets what and how much in a unit or entire organization. In this case, the head is a manager who uses the authority of the office occupied to organize how work is to be done and to assign the necessary responsibilities for goal attainment to organizational members. This is the point of prudent use of the labor of others.

Management is about coordinating the labor of others with the use of organizationally prescribed power (i.e., authority) for collective goal accomplishments. Unlike the ruler, whose authority is unbridled, the authority of the manager is limited to what the office requires for goal attainment. The restrictions of organizational policies check the authority of the manager. Unlike rulership, which grants the ruler the ability to make decisions at will and mostly without repercussions, the manager is required to make well-calculated decisions that will produce efficiency in the use of labor so as to make labor very productive. The manager can also be relieved of a position for making ineffective or inefficient decisions. This means that a manager is expected to recognize when labor is being wasted and redirect subordinates into more fruitful endeavors. In addition, in the words of Dr. Les Stein (2016), "...management is the application of social scientific principles with a focus on planning, organizing, directing, and controlling" (p.22). These are the same major organizational functions over which the manager is expected to preside, as mentioned by Gardner (2000). They are typical activities that define management.

What is Leadership?

How about leadership? How is leadership different from ruling and management? As the head, one may use leadership, rather than rulership or management, to coordinate the efforts of others toward goal attainment. Like management, leadership can, and has been, defined in multiple ways. As stated by Stogdill (1974), there are as many definitions of leadership as there are people defining the concept. Consistent with the claim by Stogdill (1974), Bennis and Nanus (1985) asserted that researchers had defined leadership in over 350 different ways in the 30 years prior to their writing in 1985. Given the varieties of definitions available for leadership, Conger (1992) suggested that leadership was mostly an intuitive concept that would never generate a single agreed-upon definition. However, regardless of the definitions used, the central theme in defining and describing leadership is *the use of non-coercive influence to guide a group* (be it an entire organization or any unit or sub-unit) in accomplishing specified goals.

Here, I shall offer four examples of leadership definitions from different authors. These four definitions are separated by 62 years, yet they are consistent with one another and with the assertion of Conger (1992) regarding the influencing nature of leadership. The consistency of these definitions can safely be taken as an indication of a persistent agreement among leadership scholars about the core meaning of leadership. The first defines leadership as the "*interpersonal influence* exercised in a situation, and directed, through the communication process, toward the attainment of a specified goal or goals" (Tannenbaum et al., 1961, p. 24). The second defines it as *an influence, a special form of power* that involves the ability of the leader to get voluntary compliance and a change in preference from followers over a broad range of matters (Etzioni, 1965). While Etzioni's definition appears on the surface to accurately capture the essence of leadership, his definition may be partially flawed, with the claim that leadership gets voluntary compliance from followers. A full understanding of the flaw in Etzioni's definition will become apparent in the discussion that I will present later in the fourth and fifth chapters of this book. The third definition states that leadership "is the process of *influencing people* to work toward a common goal" (Pride et al., 2008, p. 224), and the fourth indicates that leadership is the *influencing process* of leaders on followers to achieve organizational objectives through change (Lussier & Achua, 2023). I can add many more definitions to these four. But, given the similarities in the multitude of available definitions, these four are sufficient in expressing what leadership is, as well as demonstrating the consistency of *influence* as the definitive character of leadership.

Unlike rulership and management, both of which depend on power or bureaucratic authority to coordinate the activities of others, leadership focuses only on the use of non-coercive influence. Influence, however, is not bureaucratically embedded in any position, even the position of the head of an organization. All organizational positions have bureaucratically prescribed roles, including the authority to perform the roles. But, influence cannot be prescribed bureaucratically as we can with authority. To have influence requires building meaningful interpersonal relationships with subordinates and invariably transforming them into followers. This means that leadership is neither authoritative nor the use of an office to get things done, as a ruler or manager would. Instead, leadership requires the maintenance of particular interpersonal relationships that generate influence that is used to accomplish goals (Wolinski, 2023). Therefore, *leadership is the outcome of a relationship*, which, in turn, is used to produce the result of goal accomplishment. Put another way, *leadership is the process of influencing others, one's followers, in noncoercive ways through interpersonal relationships to achieve specified goals.* This definition and a more robust explanation of leadership will be discussed in Chapter Five, in which comparisons and contrasts will be made with management.

CHAPTER 3

UNDERSTANDING MANAGEMENT

Organizations Determine Managers

ESSENTIALS OF MANAGEMENT FUNCTIONS AND PRINCIPLES

Understanding both management and leadership accurately is essential if an executive, a manager, or a supervisor wishes to become a leader. After all, one cannot transform, or transform into, what one does not know. If one wishes to convert from manager to leader, one must be well knowledgeable about both positions. One must, especially, first understand what management is quite well because it is the official position that one occupies in an organization.

Due to their importance in the works of Henri Fayol (1841-1925), the French mining engineer and management theorist, the functions and principles of management will be discussed in this chapter, and the characteristics of management will be discussed in Chapter Four. The order of discussion of the functions and principles has no special significance beyond the flow of presentation for ease of comprehension.

FUNCTIONS OF MANAGEMENT

A manager performs management functions, indicating that *management is about the performance of certain functions* for organizational success (Fayol, [1917] 2013). By management function, Fayol referred to the set of stable and recurring activities that a manager must perform daily in the pursuit of goal accomplishment. These activities are prescriptive by the organization, indicating what management must do, rather than proscriptive, telling what management must not do. Because of the prescriptive nature of management functions, the manager has a sort of official road map for what to do with others to achieve specified goals. This shows that management functions are necessary if an organization is to succeed. That is why organizational material resources are allocated to them for their completion. The extent of available resources allocated to organizational functions is typically positively associated with the degree of importance and urgency of performing the functions. This means that a generous allocation of resources is assigned to a management function that is ranked high in importance and urgency, and vice versa. In a sense, the achievement of management goals through management functions is sensitive to the availability and allocation of organizational resources for conducting these functions.

What specifically constitutes organizational functions? Fayol ([1917] 2013) described five major functions of management. This is one of the major contributions of Fayol to the scientific management movement that was inspired by Frederick Winslow Taylor (1856-1915) in the early twentieth century. A detailed discussion of these five functions is outside the purpose of this book, but it is necessary to recognize each of them with a brief description. They are *planning and forecasting, organizing, commanding, staffing and coordinating, and controlling.* Today, management scholars tend to identify a variety of functions ranging from three (planning, motivating, and controlling) to seven (Krishali, 2021). For example, if planning and forecasting are separated and if staffing and coordinating are also uncoupled, Fayol's five functions become seven. In some cases, Fayol's classifications are replaced with different ones, or his descriptions are given new titles. For example, it is common to see the function of command be replaced by leading or directing. As Krishali indicated, the variations in the classifications of management functions occur because management scholars differ on these functions due to the divergence in the angles or perspectives through which they studied management. But, regardless of the terminology used, the important thing is that management functions are essential activities for the success of any enterprise, and they are the same in all organizations, regardless of industry. Below is a brief description of Fayol's five functions of management.

Planning and Forecasting

By Planning, Fayol ([1917] 2013) described the process of understanding and establishing goals, as well as designing methods for achieving the goals. Forecasting is the process of assessing the current state of an organization and its current resources and subsequently determining the likelihood of achieving expected outcomes of planned activities at a specified time in the future (Fayol, [1917] 2013). Forecasting is about assessing the probability that currently known and unknown future events could bear on the realization of goals associated with planning (Fayol, [1917] 2013). These events may include actions of other organizations (like government or competitors), availability of labor, cost of labor, stability of consumer preferences, and stability and availability of organizational resources. Accurate forecasting of these events and their potential impacts on planning outcomes will guide management actions in responding to them.

Organizing

The organizing function is the process of mobilizing all resources that are necessary for achieving organizational goals and prudently allocating these resources to organizational locations where they would be acted upon for goal accomplishment (Fayol, [1917] 2013). Essentially, organizing is a crucial organizational action for both the effective and efficient attainment of organizational goals.

To organize, management must perform some key activities, beginning with enumerating all activities to be performed for goal accomplishment. This is a crucial task that must be done meticulously so that no activity is missed. If an activity is omitted, the consequence may be a shortage of resources for goal accomplishment due to a lack of resource planning and allocation for the omitted activity. It is unusual for a major operation to be omitted in the organizing process, but smaller operations can easily go under the radar of the manager and subsequently have negative impacts on goal completion. This could mean that a project is delayed while the manager scrambles for additional resources, or resources are reallocated from existing allotments, which may create an inadequacy of resources for other projects. This is why it is essential for a manager to painstakingly define every activity that must be completed for goal attainment before committing organizational resources to a goal. Planning activities culminate into budgets.

Upon careful determination of all needed activities, it is the responsibility of a manager to know the best way to group these activities for the most efficient way to manage the chain and flow of work to be performed (Krishali, 2021). It is this grouping of activities that forms the basis of how organizational divisions, departments, and sub-units are created. It is the full picture of all the grouping of these activities that form the structure of an entire organization and its units (Gibson et al., 2012). This is why we see distinct units like research and development, production, marketing, and human resources in manufacturing organizations. We may see reservations and housekeeping in hotel organizations, and we may see general admissions, emergency, pharmacy, and surgery, among others, in a hospital. Each of these units specifies the various activities and the locations of activities that are relevant to goal accomplishments by type of organization. What follows the grouping of activities is the assignment of these activities to specific organizational positions and the delegation of authority to those positions (Krishali, 2021). With the designation and delegation of activities and authority to respective organizational positions, position occupiers can use the authority of their positions to perform their assigned responsibilities.

Commanding

According to Fayol, commanding is an ordering function. The manager gives orders by issuing job instructions to subordinates (Fayol, [1917] 2013). This requires clear and precise communication to be effective and efficient. As mentioned earlier, the command function is now often expressed as directing or leading (as a misnomer), which seems less domineering or authoritative. This is, perhaps, one of the consequences of changes in modern times, where people tend to prefer terms with softer tones and connotations. The terms commanding, directing, and leading are often used interchangeably in books, although technically, leading is different from the other two, and management books usually acknowledge the difference. Directing and commanding, however, are synonyms. When directing, one uses the authority of position to marshal the actions of others to achieve a goal. As stated by George R. Terry (1977), to direct is to use power to usher a group into action for goal achievement. This description is the essence of directing. For example, John Ivancevich and Thomas Duening explained directing as the managerial function that "initiates action: issuing directives, assignments, and instructions; building an effective group of subordinates who are motivated to do what must be done; explaining procedures; issuing orders; and making sure that mistakes are corrected" (Ivancevich & Duening, 2007, p.177). By these descriptions, one can tell that both commanding and directing express the giving of instructions, ordering, or telling others what to do; therefore, the interchangeable use of commanding and directing is justifiable.

The term leading, however, seems to be a more popular replacement for commanding. This may be due to the recognition of the virtues of leadership over a harsher-sounding tone of command that is frequently associated with military and paramilitary organizations than civilian associations. For Fayol, the point of commanding is that the design of an organization typically necessitates that someone must tell another what to do before anything gets done. That was his point about the term command, which carries the same message or intent as directing. Beyond issuing instructions to others to do a job, a command may also include supervising, coordinating, and inspiring subordinates to work. In this case, inspiring others to work puts the responsibility for creating positive and motivating work environments that would encourage workers to perform well on the shoulders of managers. This process, according to Fayol ([1917] 2013), will include clear managerial communication of organizational goals, performance standards, and organizational policies to subordinates. Also, for commanding success, Fayol recommended that managers should: 1) interact with their workgroup members to know them well enough to know how to create the right motivating environment for them, 2) develop effective strategies for dealing with incompetent members, 3) avoid violations of employees contracts with their organizations, 4) regularly and periodically assess employee performance, 5) implement strategies to improve unsatisfactory performance, 6) manage by example by behaving consistently with instructions and policies of the organization, and 7) cooperate with other managers in achieving common goals (Fayol, [1917] 2013).

Staffing and Coordinating

What is staffing, and why is it a vital management function worthy of discussion? The best way to understand this function is to imagine an organization that has created many job positions and acquired plenty of resources to be used in each position. With all the positions created, the organization's structural status and role arrangements are also put in place. You are the owner of the business. Now, how do you accomplish your business goals? What do you need at this stage? People! Without people occupying and conducting the roles of the positions you have created, all you have are positions and resources. However, positions and resources will not do anything until people act upon the resources with their labor to turn them into something. This is the point of staffing. Staffing is the act of finding and placing the right people in the right positions so that they can use organizational resources to achieve organizational goals. However, staffing is not just filling empty positions in an organizational structure. It is also about continuously keeping positions filled, defining workforce expectations, actively keeping track of job requirements, providing proper training, and making sure that employees are well compensated (Koontz & O'Donnell, 1968).

Management is responsible for coordinating and channeling workers' (subordinates') activities toward goal accomplishment. Ordinarily, such goals tend to focus on the unit and organization-wide ones, but it is best when they include those of individual workers because workers take jobs to achieve their own goals. Through coordination, all activities of individual workers are aligned in harmony with one another and with those of other workers in the same unit. Also, through coordination, each employee's work activities complement one another and those of other workers through the organization's bureaucracy in a value-added chain. Coordination also allows managers to determine progress being made toward goal accomplishment, as well as recognize actual and potential obstacles that may arise in the conduct of activities for goal attainment. In a simple way, the function of coordination may be accurately described as the integration of the activities of the subordinates such that goal attainment plans are effectively and efficiently executed.

Controlling

The controlling function of management is the use of rules and regulations to guide goal attainment activities so that goals are attained consistently with expected standards (Fayol, [1917] 2013). The manager controls the activities that culminate in organizational goals to make sure that each activity remains relevant and completed according to plan. Through controlling, management can recognize, from assessments, how well organizational plans are being successfully implemented, how incremental goals are being achieved, and how well the achieved goals meet or deviate from expected standards (Fayol, [1917] 2013). When deviations from standards occur, it is through controlling that management makes reports about deviations, corrects deviations, or re-evaluates plans to determine whether a plan needs to be altered or not. Controlling also allows the manager to choose the right alterations as necessitated by observed deviations. An important aspect of assessing plans is to also design contingency plans as a backup in case an original plan has to be scrapped and replaced with a different one. When a contingency plan is made simultaneously with the original plan, it reduces difficulties in modifying the original plan. According to Krishali (2021), controlling comprises three main activities: monitoring, evaluating, and correcting. Therefore, contingency plans serve as a valuable source of corrections.

One easy way to understand Fayol's stipulated five management functions may be to collapse them into three categories similar to, but differently from, the tripartite typology of planning, motivating, and controlling by Ralph. C. Davis (1951). I agree with Fayol on his first two functions, but commanding, coordinating, and controlling essentially describe different aspects of supervision. Hence, the three categories of functions that I suggest best capture all the functions of management are *planning and forecasting*, *organizing*, and *supervision*. These three categories may also be useful as a broad umbrella or paradigm for organizing various organizational functions that one may perceive.

PRINCIPLES OF MANAGEMENT

To perform management functions, a manager is expected to subscribe to certain principles known as

Management Principles or The Principles of Management (Fayol, [1917] 2013). These principles are the general guidelines rooted in certain truths, standards, or laws that should be used in managerial decisions. Adherence to management principles ensures that the performance of management functions is guided by logic and rationale rather than the unstructured whims and feelings of the manager. The outcome of the practice of these principles is the effective and efficient performance of management functions and, ultimately, achieving organizational success. The fourteen principles established by Henri Fayol underscore management decisions and behaviors for effective job performance by subordinates. Each of the fourteen principles is briefly described below.

The Principle of Division of Work

Henri Fayol used this term as a synonym for what is popularly known as the division of labor. A division of labor implies that all the activities necessary to complete the production and distribution of goods and services are divided into small components, and employees are assigned specified components to complete (Fayol, [1917] 2013).

It is important to recognize that the idea of division of work or labor did not originate with Fayol, despite the high likelihood of management students linking this concept to him because it was the first principle of management he espoused. It is also likely that the idea is perceived as originating with Frederick Taylor because it was one of the prescriptions by Taylor in his *Principles of Scientific Management* ([1911] 1997). Students of sociology or philosophy may also link this concept to Max Weber, who extensively discussed the division of labor in capitalist social institutions in his book, *The Protestant Ethic and the Spirit of Capitalism* (Weber, [1904-05] 2010). However, all these authors' conceptualizations of the division of labor have their roots in the division of labor discussed by Adam Smith. In his book, *An Inquiry into the Nature and Causes of the Wealth of Nations* (Smith, [1776] 1985), Smith included three chapters that discussed the division of labor: "Of the Division of Labor," "Of the Principle Which Gives Occasion to the Division of Labor," and "The Division of Labor is limited by the Extent of the Market" (Perackovic, 2011, pp. 1-19).

The importance of the division of labor centers around the effectiveness and efficiency of production. Take the manufacturing of cars as an example. Suppose a car manufacturing company has 10,000 workers, and each worker is trained in every detail of the manufacturing of cars. Each worker is given all the tools and resources to make a car from design to placement in the showroom. How long would it take each worker to produce one modern car with a sophisticated engine and all the bells and whistles of modern conveniences in the car? The answer will probably be the fifth day of forever! If this arduous task were achieved, it would most likely take multiple years of eight-hour weekly workdays to finish making one car. At this rate, investors who want to see some returns on their investments would probably get anxious and withdraw funding from the company. It is most likely that the company will eventually collapse. If, however, all the various tasks of the manufacturing of a car were distributed among the 10,000 workers, and each worker performed only one specialized part of the production process, it would become likely that thousands of cars could be produced each month of the year. In this case, some workers may specialize in auto design, others in bodywork, fabrications, electronics, seats, the dashboard, engine, painting, inspection, assembly, etc. With division of labor comes specialization, which will reduce time and waste of resources because, by doing the same thing regularly every day, each worker would become very good at performing one set of duties and can complete many pieces of work each day with the use of the right technology. It was through the idea of division of labor that Frederick Taylor conceived and introduced the assembly line method of production, which facilitated higher productivity in the Midville Electric Company in Cicero, Indiana, in the early 1900s (Taylor, [1911] 1997).

If one is to understand why an organization is divided into the divisions and departments that exist within it, an understanding of the division of labor is crucial. It is through the division of labor that organizational executives can determine how jobs should be grouped for effective and efficient use of organizational resources, as well as determine the location of various activities in the organization. It is through the grouping of jobs based on similarities across many dimensions, such as resources, technology, knowledge, and authority necessary to produce an outcome, that organizational units such as divisions, departments, and workgroups are created. One additional major benefit of these units is the enhancement of monitoring and supervision of organizational members by unit heads (Gibson et al., 2012).

The Principle of Authority and Responsibility

Every position in an organization is accorded some amount of organizational authority, which the occupier of a position uses to perform the duties of the position (Fayol, [1917] 2013). This use of authority is especially important for analysis because of the possibility of abuse by managers whose authority includes giving orders to others. According to Fayol, the distribution of organizational (that is, bureaucratic) authority should be carefully designed such that no position is allocated more authority than is necessary to function effectively. In allocating authority to a position, organizational executives who are responsible for authority allocation should balance position responsibilities with the necessary position authority. The right to give instructions and orders should not be more or less than is required for each position. If allocated authority substantially exceeds responsibilities, a manager could easily abuse authority. At the same time, less authority than is needed to perform responsibilities would cause frustrations and job dissatisfaction for the manager. Hence, an optimum balance of authority and responsibilities should be observed as an essential management principle (Fayol, [1917] 2013).

The Principle of Discipline

If managers have the authority to give orders, subordinates are obligated to obey the orders as part of the conditions for membership in an organization (Fayol, [1917] 2013). The rules, regulations, guidelines, and policies of an organization or unit are communicated through management, and members are expected to act according to these rules. This means that organizational members should exercise self-discipline to obey all organizational rules. Otherwise, they risk being punished by their manager on behalf of the organization. This is the point of discipline as a management principle. It is a management tool that requires organizational rules to be respected and followed through self or organizationally-imposed discipline on all organizational members. In a manager-subordinate relationship, discipline guidelines are exercised downwards from the manager to the subordinate, who must perform as instructed by the manager or face disciplinary actions from the manager.

The principle of discipline also requires that organizational rules not be bent to accommodate employee behavior, and management, too, must not apply rules with partiality. If, for example, organizational members are expected to exercise self-discipline to be at their seats by 9:00 am, those who show up late are expected to be uniformly sanctioned for the same rule violation. The organization should not change its rules regarding punctuality to accommodate tardiness by some members. To do so will violate the principle of discipline. It may also encourage further tardiness from nonconforming members, as well as risk disapproval and dissent from rule-abiding members.

I was once contacted by a church elder who wanted my opinion on how to get members of his small church to be punctual. His church membership was mostly people from his West African country. Members were regularly showing up for Sunday services about two hours late, and the church pastor would wait till the members arrived before commencing service. I asked him why the pastor delayed services rather than starting on time. He answered that if service started on time, the members would miss their needed prayers, and the church would also lose financial donations for the week. Without the weekly donations, the church would not be able to pay its bills. This puts the church between the proverbial rock and a hard place. The church was in a predicament with either choice of action it might take. To start on time was to lose money, and to start late was to condone and even unwillingly facilitate tardiness. The church had already condoned and enabled tardiness to get its weekly donations. It had bent its rules, and it had enabled indiscipline. It wanted to reimpose discipline, but it found itself in a conundrum between its two interests.

To avoid such a paradox as faced by the church in the previous paragraph, Fayol indicated that the principle of discipline, like the other management principles, should not be compromised. Like any other organization, the church, in my example, should adhere to the principle of discipline by observing its own rules. In conformity with the principle of discipline, I advised the church elder to convince his clergy to start services on time as scheduled, even at the likely expense of some members missing portions of a service or missing a service entirely. It may also mean losing some Sunday donations. I was later informed that the church began to adhere to the principle of discipline, which eventually spurred the members to arrive on time for service every Sunday. It eventually became the norm for the church to regularly hold its services on time with its full congregation.

The Principle of Unity of Command

Fayol ([1917] 2013) specified this principle so that managers could avoid the dual subordination of any worker. According to Fayol, each worker must take instructions from only one manager and report to only one manager, normally the one to whom the worker regularly reports by organizational design. No worker must, by structural design, report to more than one manager. This means that no worker must be compelled to have two or more managers at the same time for any position occupied in an organization. As a structural standard, this also means that every worker is expected to be a part of only one command group at a time.

When properly followed, unity of command helps to prevent many problems for workers, managers, and the organization. A worker who reports to more than one manager may face many issues, such as different expectations for performance standards, possibly having to deal with contradictory instructions, incompatible job demands, being overworked, anxiety in meeting the demands of two different sets of expectations (especially when the expectations are incongruent), and anxiety over performance evaluations by various managers. The multiple managers to whom an employee reports may also clash over their use of the employee's time, especially when the employee is unable to complete a task assignment for one manager due to the time devoted to a project assigned by another. In the end, the organization itself may suffer from the possible poor performance of the employee, caused, at least in part, by role conflicts from membership in more than one command group.

The Principle of Unity of Direction

For organizational efficiency, Fayol ([1917] 2013) reasoned that organizations would achieve efficiency if organizational activities with the same end goals were organized under the supervision of one manager. This manager would devise and implement one central plan for how to conduct the activities that lead to the achievement of the goals. In a way, unity of direction is the process of having one manager take responsibility for devising and implementing a plan to streamline job processes with a single design for completing the various tasks, as well as coordinating the efforts of workers for the achievement of a goal. Unity of direction can also be viewed as "rowing in the same direction," as one former department chairman in my university used to urge members of the department. This comment was in an attempt to get everyone in the department committed to a common vision and shared activities needed to achieve any particular departmental goal. So, as an example, to conduct a successful marketing campaign for a new product, the principle of unity of direction will require that all activities for marketing, such as packaging, branding, advertising, promotions, pricing, sales, distribution, etc., be under one executive who must make one comprehensive plan for the execution of all these activities. This does not preclude having supervisors or coordinators for each area of the labor division needed to accomplish marketing goals. It only means that the head of marketing should oversee the design of the comprehensive marketing plan that unifies all the activities that must be completed in each subdivision of the grand plan.

The Principle of Subordination of Individual Interest

Fayol ([1917] 2013) indicated that management requires training the individual worker to make the priorities of the general organization first, and those of the individual second, in all matters relating to organizational success. This principle acknowledges the importance of individual interests but only as a secondary priority to those of the organization. An individual joins an organization for personal interests such as making an income, having power, prestige, respect, and keeping busy. While individual interests may drive an employee to show up for work, the individual is expected to put the general interest of the success of the organization first. It is when the organization succeeds that it can reward its members as well as retain them. Hence, organizational goals must supersede personal goals. The order of the importance of interests between the individual and the general organization should not be a subject of debate. However, ignorance, ambition, selfishness, laziness, weakness, and passion often cause workers to place their personal interests above those of the organization (Fayol, [1917] 2013). Such misplacement of interests is in error and counterproductive to employee well-being. It is detrimental to the workers as they will eventually suffer from a lack of adequate rewards when the organization fails to generate enough resources to adequately reward them.

Fayol's ideas equally apply to understanding the subordination of general organizational interests to those of smaller units and groups within an organization. Organizational units are expected to make organizational goals a priority, and they are expected to set unit goals as a subsidiary of organizational goals. This way, the accomplishments of unit goals will directly contribute to the achievement of organizational goals. This principle is, however, easily violated as organizational units often hold greater allegiance to their own units than to the entire organization (Gibson et al., 2012). This is especially true when organizations are designed around functional departmentalization, whereby workers are grouped into departments based on their specialized skills and functions in an organization. This type of organizational structural design has been observed to place allegiance to the unit over allegiance to the organization (Gibson et al., 2012). For example, because of functional departmentalization, cardiologists and ophthalmologists may place greater allegiance to the goals of the cardiology and ophthalmology departments, respectively, over those of their hospitals in general. Such allegiance is detrimental to the organization because it can hinder or even sabotage organizational goals and, hence, poses a challenge to organizational success.

The Principle of Remuneration

Remuneration is the compensation an organization gives its workers for their labor. It is a payment made to workers in exchange for their labor (Fayol, [1917] 2013). While an organization will undoubtedly benefit from the labor of a worker, Fayol indicated that the system of reward in an organization must be fair. The principle of remuneration, therefore, centers around fairness through equity. Fayol stated that each organization should have a system of rewards that is fair to both the employee and the organization.

As Frederick Herzberg and his colleagues put it, because financial rewards are hygiene factors that only reduce dissatisfaction rather than create motivation, employees should be well compensated for their labor sufficiently not to be dissatisfied with their organization

(Herzberg et al., 1959). But payments need not be only financial. Fayol mentioned that the remuneration principle should comprise both financial and non-financial compensations, which should be used as performance incentives. It is important, as Fayol indicated, that compensation should be designed as a system. Systems produce consistency, hence making it possible to fairly reward organizational members based on job performance and the capacity of the organization to reward on a consistent basis. The compensation system should also be designed to encourage eagerness without overpayments. To do this, workers could be paid at time rates, job rates, or piece rates, and when applicable, bonuses and profit-sharing could be included in the remuneration system (Fayol, [1917] 2013).

The Principle of Centralization

Centralization is a measure of the extent of authority distribution in an organization (Fayol, [1917] 2013). When authority is mostly concentrated at or near the top positions in an organization, the organization is described as having high centralization, low decentralization, or low delegation (Tolbert & Hall, 2016). When authority is widely distributed across all levels of positions, especially supervisory positions, the organization is described as having low centralization, high decentralization, or high delegation (Tolbert & Hall, 2016).

Authority distribution is inherent to the functioning of any organization. An organization cannot exist without distributing authority to the different positions in which organizational activities must be performed. A 100 percent centralization cannot exist in an organization because, among other reasons, top executives must give some amount of power to other managers and supervisors, as well as every worker, so that all organizational members will have the necessary authority to perform their duties. At the same time, an organization cannot survive with 100 percent decentralization. Top executives and managers still need the essential authority to control the organization and steer it in the direction necessary for its survival. According to Fayol, the question regarding centralization is not whether organizational authority should be distributed because distribution is unavoidable. The question is about what amount should be distributed and to whom. This question is not easily answered because many factors play a part in the distribution of authority to subordinates.

The factors that shape the distribution of organizational authority include what the organization does, the size of the organization, the technology being used to perform tasks, the complexity of the organizational structure, top management's perceptions of workers, the complexity of knowledge needed to perform tasks, and the characteristics of organizational members in terms of education, professional status, skills level, etc. A full discussion of each of these factors is outside the description of the centralization principle in this book. What is important, however, is that the principle of centralization indicates that the distribution of organizational authority requires a good balance between centralization and decentralization. Authority distribution to the various levels of an organization should reflect the characteristics of the organization and the amount of authority necessary for the successful performance of duties. And while management retains the authority to make final decisions, subordinates should also be given adequate authority to do their jobs.

The Principle of the Scalar Chain

The principle of the scalar chain, or the scalar principle, was Fayol's description of the system of a chain of command that is built into every organizational structure.

Every organizational structure shows the lines of communication and authority that flow downwards from the top to the bottom of an organization (Fayol, [1917] 2013). It is the appearance of these lines, as they vertically link one position to the other, that gives the principle its name as a chain. Along the lines of a chain are command or management positions that stipulate who gives commands to whom; hence, the scalar principle is consistent with the unity of command principle, as it shows only one manager for each command group on the scalar chain.

Aside from indicating who gives orders to whom, the central element of the scalar principle is respect for the bureaucratic protocol, which requires instructions to flow downwards to subordinates through their managers. Also, in the reverse, any communication or feedback to higher management should flow upwards through the managers (Fayol, [1917] 2013). This principle, therefore, stipulates that a higher manager should not bypass a lower manager and issue directives to the lower manager's subordinates. Likewise, the subordinates cannot sidestep their managers and go to higher managers to pitch an idea or complain about the organization or even their managers. Any idea or complaint that subordinates have must go through their immediate managers for redress, and only their managers can forward the ideas and complaints to higher managers. When subordinates sidestep their immediate manager and go to a higher manager to seek redress of a grievance or pitch an idea, adherence to the scalar principle requires the higher manager to send subordinates back to their manager to commence the pitching of an idea or redress of a grievance, even when a complaint is about one's manager.

A very important aspect of the scalar principle, aside from respect for the chain of command, is the quality of decisions that are made based on the clarity of the command chain. When the command chain is very clear and precise, and when it is strictly followed, the centers of decision-making become clear. Everyone in an organization would know who makes what decisions and who to contact for various choices. Decisions are also made more effectively and efficiently when it is clear where decisions are to be made about different activities in an organization. This type of clearness in decision-making facilitated by the chain of command is one of the benefits of the mechanical organizational structure, which eliminates confusion, ambiguity, anomie, and, consequently, deviant behavior (Burns & Stalker, 1961). If the chain of command is not clear and the scalar principle is not enforced, confusion may easily arise about who is heading a command group and whose instructions workers should obey. This will increase the chances of workers violating expected organizational standards for behavior. These facts are important considerations for adherence to the rules of the scalar chain as a management principle.

The Principle of Order

Every organization must maintain order, and it begins with placing everyone and everything in their respective logical and rational places within the structure of an organization (Fayol, [1917] 2013). That is the central point of the principle of order. An organization must be orderly to function well and attain its goals, and this requires managers to place material resources, technology, and tools (that is, things) where they belong for effective use in organizational performance. Organizational members and resources, alike, must occupy only the place designed for them in an organizational structure. This means that managers must wisely allocate people to the right places where they can best perform. These placements express the essence of two forms of order: Material Order and Social Order.

In material order, the principle of order indicates there is a right and a wrong place for organizational materials, and it is the duty of managers to place materials in their right places. For social order, people are to be placed in the right places for job performance. For both material and social order to be effectively performed, managers must know the right materials for their organization and only purchase those materials (Fayol, [1917] 2013). In the same regard, management must hire only the right people based on organizational needs for job performance. This means that organizational needs must first be determined before an employee is hired and placed rather than the reverse order, which may happen as a result of mismanagement. Also, managers must not procure the wrong materials because there will be no right location for them, and the wrong people should not be hired because there will be no right location to place them.

If the wrong materials are procured and placed in an organization or if the wrong people are employed and placed in the organizational structure, a disorder will occur. The wrong materials and the wrong people cannot be effectively and efficiently used, thereby creating resource wastage for the organization. If forced into production, the wrong materials will destroy the production process, and the wrong people will be ineffective and inefficient in conducting their responsibilities (Fayol, [1917] 2013). Both of these scenarios will also be costly to an organization and raise the organization's production cost (Fayol, [1917] 2013). This is why the principle of order is very important. Misplacements are costly to organizations as they create disorder.

The Principle of Equity

Equity as a management principle focuses on two main practices: kindness and justice (Fayol, [1917] 2013). Fayol indicated that when dealing with subordinates, managers should use both kindness and justice equally. This position assumes that kindness and justice are equally important to achieve equity. Do you accept this premise by Henri Fayol, or do you think, in your logical analysis, that one is more important than the other? Fayol suggested that the practice of kindness and justice would not only produce equity but also create loyalty and commitment to the organization. I think a brief analysis and disagreement with Fayol are appropriate at this time.

Without a doubt, kindness is a good thing. No one would argue that management should be unkind to workers. What constitutes kindness to subordinates, however, may be contested. This is because equity requires equal fairness to all. If fairness is equally given out to every subordinate, the question of kindness becomes moot. If the rules of an organization are fairly and equally applied, justice will prevail in the organization. However, if organizational rules are bent for kindness, the principle of discipline, which requires management not to bend the rules, gets violated. The principle of discipline requires workers to discipline themselves to abide by organizational rules, perhaps on the assumption that the rules would be fair, and therefore, nullifying any need for special kindness.

Another way to think of equity as nullifying kindness is to see it from the perspective of material remuneration or distributive justice. According to John Stacey Adams (1963, 1965), equity in remuneration occurs when the reward for the ratio of input to output of one employee is proportional to those of similarly employed workers. For example, assume that John and Mary occupy similar positions, and they are subordinates to Adam. At the end of the month, John worked 160 hours and got paid $3,200, and Mary worked 180 hours and got paid $3,600. Here, equity is achieved between the two employees. Each employee was paid $20 per hour worked, the prevailing wage for their positions, so the difference in their end-of-the-month wages was the result of the number of hours each person worked. In this case, kindness is unnecessary, and it is unlikely that either employee would complain of injustice.

Let us consider the above scenario from another angle. Suppose John is having some financial difficulties in his personal life, and Adam shows kindness to John by paying him $3,600 rather than the $3,200 he has earned. In that case, this act of kindness to John violates the principle of equity and treats Mary with injustice. While John may be happy and grateful to Adam, Mary will be justified in being angry and complaining of injustice, among other possible complaints she might have against Adam. This is one reason structurally designed justice is more important than kindness. This is not to imply that managers should be unkind to their subordinates. The point here is that kindness is questionable and unnecessary as an equity factor. This is because equity is expected as a structurally produced justice, not kindness. But, because kindness is also a good virtue, there should be a place for it in managerial actions. Perhaps it deserves to be recognized and developed as a separate managerial principle.

The Principle of Stability of Tenure

This principle states that employees should be retained for a reasonable amount of time before being dismissed for incompetence. Management should provide room for employment stability in the best interest of an organization (Fayol, [1917] 2013). Workers who are new to their jobs need time to learn the demands and competencies of their jobs because competence does not occur instantly, like instant coffee. Therefore, this principle suggests that a new employee should not be sacked too quickly due to ineffective or inefficient performance. It takes time for any employee to understand the nuances of a job and to become very effective and efficient in doing it. Depending on how well a job is designed, the mastery of a job may take a long or a short period, but some amount of learning time is expected to become competent. According to the principle of stability of tenure of personnel, management should be aware of the learning time requirement for jobs and provide necessary resources, especially training, which would aid the worker in becoming good at a job.

There are benefits to both an employee and an organization when the stability of tenure of personnel principle is followed. When an employee has the opportunity to learn a job very well, the job is likely to be done efficiently. If all other factors remain constant, the employee will likely stay with the organization for a long time and develop a career within the organization. The efficiency derived from long-term tenure and career growth in the same organization will save the organization plenty of money in the long run. The efficiency of the worker would translate into higher revenues for the organization as the worker generates high productivity from long-term experience, assuming other factors do not mitigate the benefits of long tenure. Also, the long-term commitment and career growth would translate into profits from low turnover savings generated by not having to hire new workers, training them, and enduring a period of low productivity. By granting employees the time to learn their jobs, the stability of tenure provides employment longevity that benefits organizations.

The Principle of Initiative

The principle of initiative indicates that management should grant all levels of supervision and staff the room to initiate and carry out their plans (Fayol, [1917] 2013). This is expected to promote creativity among workers. Fayol indicated that management should encourage workers to show initiative without being restricted by supervisory authority.

The creativity that employee initiatives would produce is considered a potential source of growth for an organization. Such initiatives would spur commitment to action from the employees and consequently boost their levels of job satisfaction. The principle of initiative, therefore, implies the need for greater decentralization of authority in an organization. If initiatives are to occur without supervisory authority restrictions, managers and supervisors must relinquish some authority to subordinates for their creative thinking and suggestions of new ideas to alter customary prevailing job processes.

When managers and supervisors feel threatened by relinquishing some authority to workers, a limitation is placed on the ability of workers to exhibit creativity, and the principle of initiative is truncated or, at worst, becomes null and void. To effectively use this principle, top management should create a culture that rewards creativity and rewards managers and supervisors whose teams take the initiative to creatively perform their jobs.

The Principle of Esprit De Corps

Esprit de corps concerns the positive spirit of working together as a group (Fayol, [1917] 2013). This is because work is a social event in which workers interact with one another in their respective units to achieve individual and unit goals. The process of work brings people together, interacting with one another and achieving common objectives. As demonstrated by Elton Mayo and his colleagues (1946) in the Hawthorne Experiment, team spirit is a major source of job performance. However, team spirit does not occur without a stimulus. It requires something to ignite it. In the Hawthorne experiment, esprit de corps was ignited by the attention that workers received during the study to understand some environmental factors of employee performance. Attention was the external stimulus. The workers at the Western Electric plant where the study was conducted said the attention given to them by being watched as research participants was unique, and it gave them a feeling of importance. The attention was not only effective as a stimulus for the esprit de corps with the experimental group but also with the control group, as both groups increased their output during the experiment (Mayo et al., 1946).

Fayol explained that the manager is responsible for creating a social environment for unity and cooperation that generates esprit de corps (team spirit) among workers. Esprit de corps produces harmony and cohesion among workers, and the organization gains strong and committed teams.

Fayol warned against the use of divide-and-conquer policies of supervision because such policies create disunity and dysfunctional conflicts. Such policies will mostly weaken an organization, even if individual managers gain power through conquest. Likely outcomes of disunity include dislike of fellow workers and the manager, anger, alienation from coworkers, and attrition or a strong desire for it. But when esprit de corps is nurtured, the strength in the association among workers will generate high productivity for the betterment of an organization and all members, including managers, so it is a principle to uphold rather than divide and rule behaviors (Fayol, [1917] 2013).

CHAPTER 4

BEHAVIORAL CHARACTERISTICS OF MANAGEMENT

Managers and Subordinates Are Formal Organizational Positions.

Managers Do Things Right!

IDEAL-TYPE MANAGEMENT CHARACTERISTICS

In this chapter, I shall outline the characteristics of management so that we can differentiate leadership from management in the next chapter. It is the performance of these behavioral characteristics that makes the head of a group a manager. While Chapter Three focuses on the roles of management in terms of its functions and principles, this chapter describes the behavioral patterns (or characteristics) that define the manager. The behavioral characteristics will be the ideal-type.

The concept of ideal-type, as used by Max Weber ([1904-05] 2010), implies that there are several characteristics that we can use to describe a phenomenon. But, when comparing and contrasting two or more phenomena, only the essential characteristics or a standard statistical average of each phenomenon should be used. Essential or standard statistical averages form the ideal-type characteristics of any phenomenon (Weber, [1904-05] 2010). For example, if we wish to describe a human being, the ideal-type characteristics of human beings will include one head, hair on the head, two eyes, one nose, two ears, two arms, ten fingers, two legs, and ten toes. These are ideal-type characteristics of humans because they represent the essential or standard average of physical features that humans typically possess. But we are also fully aware that some humans are naturally bald, and some are born with only one ear, some have only one eye or no eyes at all, some are born with only one leg, others with only one arm, and the number of fingers and toes may vary. While those with varied features are still humans, the ideal-type characteristics give us the most accurate typical description of a human being compared to the variations of the characteristics. This is why the ideal-type characteristics will be adopted for a good understanding of managerial behaviors in this chapter and for contrasting them with leadership in the next chapter.

In the interest of brevity and the high likelihood that the reader of this book would already have some familiarity with management either through experience, job training, or academic learning, only eight ideal-type characteristics of management that shape managerial behaviors will be discussed in this chapter. As mentioned earlier, the ideal-type does not imply *only,* but rather, the most essential or most typical features that define a situation. The eight ideal-type characteristics discussed below are deemed sufficient to accurately portray management and the manager in contrast with leadership and the leader.

Goal Orientation

A key feature of management is goal orientation (Brevis, 2014). It is a straightforward fact that the main purpose of management is to achieve organizational goals with the least amount of labor and other resources (Barnard, 1938). So, by definition, management is a process of coordinating the efforts or the labor of others toward goal accomplishments. When this coordination is done well, it is effective and efficient. However, this need not be the case for management to occur. The point of management is the coordination of the labor or productive activities of others regardless of its extent of effectiveness and efficiency, though ordinarily, high effectiveness and efficiency are preferred and expected by organizational bureaucracy. It is inherent in management that the series of activities and processes involved in goal attainment be effectively and efficiently accomplished by organizational bureaucratic design. The manager, therefore, is the person charged with this responsibility of coordination for effective and efficient goal attainment.

Management goals can be described in two broad types. The first is the *instrumental type* (Parsons, 1966). Instrumental goals are designed as *directly intended management outcomes*. They are the specific goals that an organization must achieve to stay in business. For example, a bank must sell loans, make profits from loan interests and other investments, have deposits, and increase the number of its customers, among many other goals. In other words, a bank must achieve multiple goals if it is to stay in business, and it must hire managers to coordinate the labor of other workers to achieve these goals. These goals form the reason for having management positions and hiring managers. That is, the coordination of resources and the efforts of others to attain instrumental goals are the reasons for having managers in organizations.

Instrumental goals will vary depending on the mission and activities of an organization. For example, the goals of a university are decidedly different from those of a manufacturing organization. While the overarching goal of the university may be the provision of quality education, that of the manufacturing organization may be the production of high-quality physical products like automobiles, computers, clothes, or furniture. The managerial activities of the director of admissions at a university may include coordinating the efforts of admissions officers in enrolling a target number of qualified students. But, the management goals for a human resource manager at the manufacturing corporation may include periodic safety training of all employees in the production line. Because these instrumental goal expectations determine the reasons for the existence of management, they also form the criteria upon which the effectiveness of a manager is measured. In addition, because rewards are tied to performance effectiveness, the effective performance of instrumental goals becomes the ultimate basis for determining managerial rewards.

The second type of goal is described as the *expressive type* (Parsons, 1966). Expressive goals focus mainly on the *general well-being* of workers. These goals may include the concern for the well-being of subordinates in and out of the workplace. That may mean that management responsibilities include making sure the manager provides a friendly work environment, creating opportunities for workers to be socially involved with one another, as well as creating a work environment where workers feel comfortable getting help from one another and supporting one another emotionally. A manager's expressive roles may also include fostering camaraderie among subordinates, soothing hurt feelings, encouraging humor, and handling conflict (Crossman, 2020) to make the workgroup emotionally satisfying for all workers. Off work, the manager may also maintain an expressive goal that caters to the physical and mental health of workers. Showing concern for employee family discomforts and showing positive interest in the general welfare of employees are also expressive goals within the concerns of a manager.

While management goals may include expressive ones, managers are hardly rewarded for achieving them. Expressive goals are rarely, if ever, assessed as part of a manager's overall job performance. This may be partially due to the expectation that the outcome of a good work environment will be evident in a group's output that will be high in both quality and quantity. With this assumption, an organization's assessment structure may focus on measuring a manager's performance through instrumental goals alone. In fact, expressive goals can be fully ignored, regardless of how well a manager may achieve them, if instrumental goals are not achieved. For example, a bank manager will be laid off if a bank is not profitable, regardless of how well the manager has achieved expressive goals. Similarly, a football coach will be dismissed, even before the end of a league season, if a team has lost all its games, even when expressive functions are well achieved.

Given the predominance of organizational desire to achieve instrumental goals, managers are forced to direct their efforts to achieve these goals. It is a safe and rational option for managers because they are more likely to be rewarded for achieving instrumental goals than expressive ones. Hence, while they achieve instrumental goals, they often do so in an atmosphere of poor human relations within their workgroups. This is a common trade-off that typifies managerial behavior.

Manager-Subordinate Relations

Another ideal characteristic of management is that a manager has subordinates. This is an important characteristic of being a manager to keep in mind. Given that a manager is given the responsibility to coordinate the efforts of others towards common goals, managerial status inherently signifies an organizationally structured hierarchy of relationships between one person and others. This indicates that *managers have an inbuilt hierarchical relationship with those in their span of control.* These are the subordinates who report to any particular manager. They are a manager's workgroup, which is technically referred to as the manager's *command group* (Gibson et al., 2012). They take instructions from the manager to perform work for the completion of specific tasks assigned to them. All manners of relationships between the manager and the command group are specified in the job descriptions of each worker, and they are typically written into an organization's operations manual as dictated by the extent of organizational formalization.

Two important facts about the manager and a command group are that the relationship between the two is officially prescribed in an organizational structure, and command group members are fully under the authority of their manager. Whether command group members like or dislike their manager does not change the fact that all of them remain subordinates to the manager. By organizational design, all members of a manager's command group are bound to take all legitimate instructions from the manager and meet his expectations for job performance.

Bureaucratic Authority: Authorized Power

Managers are bureaucratically required to rely on the use of bureaucratic authority, a variant of power that is rooted in the authority of position, to coordinate the actions of their subordinates (Dornbusch & Scott, 1975). Bureaucratic authority is the *authorized power* granted by organizational bureaucracy (Weber, 1947). As stated earlier, every position in an organizational structure is designed with some amount of rational-legal authority necessary for job performance. This authority is also described as *job depth* (Gibson et al., 2012; Ivancevic et al., 2014). It is inherent in managers' positions that they have organizationally allocated authority for issuing instructions and coordinating the work of their subordinates. With authority comes sanctions: rewards for conformity and punishments for nonconformity (Watson, 1930). The manager can use the authority of her position to tell her command group what to do and expect obedience from each group member. Authorized power is a top-down power system that compels subordinates to obey managerial commands (Fayol, [1917] 2013; Weber, 1947) and thereby demands from the employees a zone of indifference in which managerial authority can be successfully exercised.

The amount of authority a manager commands depends on the location of the position occupied in an organizational structure and the tallness of the structure (Bacharach & Lawler, 1980). Normally, organizational size shapes managerial power. When an organization is very large and has a tall structure, the taller the structure and the higher the level of managerial position, the greater the amount of authority embedded in the position (Bacharach & Lawler, 1980). The amount of authority allocated to a position also determines the extent to which a manager can issue directives and give sanctions. The most important thing to know here is that to get things done, authorized power is the basis for the actions of managers. Managers rely on the authority of their positions in dealing with their subordinates and for the response that they expect from the subordinates.

Response to managerial authority by subordinates may extend beyond the formal boundaries of the workplace. It may also apply when managers and subordinates interact in social events away from the workplace. Both managers and subordinates have been socialized through organizational bureaucracy to recognize the dimension of power and power outcomes between them. So, in off-the-job interpersonal relations, subordinates mostly continue to respect the job authority of the manager and continue to subordinate themselves to the manager. Subordinates usually still feel an organizationally induced pressure and compulsion to defer to the manager in areas in which they may hold different opinions from the manager and also act consistently with the authority of the manager. For example, the subordinate may run personal errands for the manager, listen to the manager without interruptions, and even laugh at the manager's dry jokes. This occurs as a result of workplace manager-subordinate relations that carry over to the off-the-job arena, in which the subordinate ought to be independent of the manager's workplace authority.

In a way, the subordinate is always under the pressure of the manager's authority and the potential consequences of the real or assumed threat of the authority in and out of the workplace. This constant threat of the authority of management underscores the ability of the manager to coordinate the work of subordinates and get obedient compliance from them.

Obedient Compliance by Subordinates

The expected response from the use of managerial authority over the subordinates is obedient compliance! A Manager gets work done by getting obedient compliance from subordinates regardless of their differing opinions and intent to resist the manager (Dornbusch & Scott, 1975). A manager is authorized to issue directives to subordinates, and subordinates, in turn, are obligated, as designed by organizational bureaucracy, to act according to the directives. For any organization or its units to work in an orderly manner, subordinates are compelled by organizational rules, policies, and culture to abide by the directives of their managers. All directives from a manager are required to be obeyed, as laws are obeyed in society. Citizens are expected to obey all laws without the option to choose which ones to obey or not obey (Postema, 2001; Sevel, 2018).

Like laws, subordinates are not at liberty under organizational rules to refuse compliance with management's instructions, nor are they allowed to pick and choose which management directives to obey or ignore. Even at upper levels of organizational positions, higher executives expect and demand obedience from their subordinates, who, themselves, are also high-level executives. The president of a corporation expects compliance from the vice president, as the vice president expects compliance from senior managers, and this pattern of expectations for compliance with directives goes in this systematic manner to the bottom of the scalar chain.

The concept of compliance indicates one's obedience to acting according to rules, standards, or instructions. It means one is forced to obey rules and act according to the terms of a rule, policy, guideline, or instruction from a superior officer. Compliance with a manager's directives, therefore, is not based on voluntary expectations. It is based on expectations for self-submission through rational-legal coercion. This is why the term obedient compliance is appropriate in describing a subordinate's favorable response to managerial directives.

Going back to the rational legality of each position in an organizational structure, the position of management is a rationally and legally recognized position to coordinate the labor of subordinates and, in doing so, to give instructions to subordinates to obey. The ability of the manager to give instructions and expect them to be followed is rooted in organizational backing for the authority of the manager to issue directives. By the same token, subordinates are, by rational legality, required to obey the directives and act as required of them to provide the means to the end determined by the manager. Obedience is not a willing action. It is a required action. It is induced mainly through fear of perceived or actual punishment for not obeying or through perceived or actual reward for obeying. This shows, at least in part, that management is not inherently, by design, a friendly process. Instead, it is a coercive approach based on rules and sanctions for the accomplishment of organizational instrumental goals. This suggests another reason managerial efforts are more likely to be directed at instrumental goals than expressive ones.

Management Techniques

As an ideal characteristic, managers employ management techniques to coordinate the efforts of their subordinates toward goal accomplishment. These techniques are analytical and systematic methods used by managers to guide decision-making for effective and efficient organizational performance, particularly in planning and control (Armstrong, 2003). In other words, the achievement of organizational goals, the conduct of managerial functions, and the practice of management principles are all facilitated through a series of methods collectively known as management techniques. Unlike management functions and principles, which are well-defined within limited specified parameters by Fayol ([1917] 2013), management techniques are numerous. Any managerial method used to achieve goals technically qualifies as a management technique. This abundance of techniques poses a challenge in discussing them comprehensively, as it is unlikely to cover the endless list of potential management techniques in a single discussion. For this book, the description of management techniques will primarily be drawn from *"A Handbook of Management Techniques,"* a bestselling guide to modern management methods by Michael Armstrong (2003).

Michael Armstrong indicated that management techniques depend on the area of management under consideration. For example, in the area of *general management*, which focuses mainly on planning and control, the most important management technique is planning. In the area of *marketing management*, management techniques such as market research, forecasting, product analysis, product planning, pricing, and sales are most crucial. *Operations management*, which relies heavily on the use of computers, requires the techniques of planning, scheduling, and product and service control. In the *financial management area,* managers rely mainly on analytical techniques that involve planning, budgeting, and control. In the area of *human resource management*, Armstrong listed techniques that included human resource planning, salary and compensation administration, performance appraisal, training, and management development. He also listed techniques such as data processing for *information technology* activities, and to achieve *organizational effectiveness and efficiency,* he listed audit, cost reduction, profit improvement, work-study, and productivity planning methods (Armstrong, 2003).

Management techniques are also perceived in other ways differently from Armstrong's descriptions and, in some cases, include management styles. Unfortunately, because of the lack of a thorough understanding of leadership, management techniques are often described as leadership techniques or styles. This is true in management consulting and in management and leadership books that many management students read. The three main forms of management techniques that are often mislabeled as leadership styles are authoritative, participative, and laissez-faire. I will briefly discuss them here.

Authoritative Management Technique. As the name implies, this technique involves the use of organizationally prescribed authority as a straight command in the coordination of the labor of others to get work done. This method is the main tool of control in rulership, which was discussed in Chapter Two; hence, when a manager is authoritative or dictatorial, he assumes the status of a ruler and treats his subordinates as subjects. If organizational bureaucracy permits authoritarianism, the manager's subordinates, in effect, become his subjects. Like rulership, managers who use this method dictate to others what to do and expect straight obedience from them. Because the authoritative style has been sufficiently discussed under rulership, it will not be fully discussed again here. The reader is encouraged to review the discussion of rulership in

Chapter Two and transfer knowledge from there to this section. That said, a few additional comments will be made here regarding the authoritative management technique.

Except for some special occasions where it is effective and valuable, as mentioned in Chapter Two, authoritativeness is viewed as counterproductive in most instances, and it is best to avoid it whenever possible. Subordinates who are subjected to authoritarianism will mostly find this method of workgroup governance abusive, disrespectful, and humiliating. Their ability to make good subjective decisions that could improve the organization is mostly unrecognized or ignored. This is evident in the observation that when workers disapprove of the power distance between them and the authoritative manager, their productivity typically falls (Schaubroeck et al., 2017). The disapproval may also easily breed contempt for the manager and result in bad organizational citizenship behaviors (OCB) and incivility toward the manager and the organization. The contempt and its consequences may additionally stem from the constraints that an authoritarian manager puts on workers' initiatives and critical thinking (see Purwanto et al., 2020). It may also be the result of the neglect of workers' needs because the authoritarian manager engages in one-directional communication with the workers, which prevents him from knowing their needs and catering to them. Therefore, he loses value as someone the workers could count on to help them achieve their individual goals, as expressed in the wisdom of the Path-Goal Theory (see House, 1971).

Authoritarianism should be avoided by managers who value freedom or opportunities to contribute to work processes (Anisa, 2020). It is also especially important to avoid authoritative commands when dealing with highly skilled, well-educated, and professional subordinates. These classes of workers typically do non-routine conceptual jobs that require complex knowledge and non-routine technology. Built into their positions is a fair amount of organizationally granted discretionary authority necessary to perform their duties (Tolbert & Hall, 2016). A manager who attempts to use authoritarianism over these workers would likely be rebuffed at the very least and, at worst, become involved in direct clashes with them (Gibson et al., 2012; Tolbert & Hall, 2016). This class of workers, therefore, is best managed through either a form of participative management or a laissez-faire technique.

The Participative Management Technique.
In participative management, the manager and the subordinates work together to achieve a unit's objectives. Both the manager and the subordinates engage in collaborative efforts to get work done. This method comprises two dimensions of decision-making: a consultative approach and a group or democratic approach (Halloran & Benton, 1987). The *consultative approach* describes the situation whereby managers speak to each member of their command group individually, collectively, or both to solicit their suggestions on a decision to be made. The manager may ask questions from the command group about the decision to be made and listen to the key points that are raised on both sides of the question. After consultations, the manager makes independent decisions and informs the command group about his decisions based on the input of the group. In the *group* or *democratic approach,* the manager sits with the command group, discusses an issue with the group, and actively participates in a collective decision with the group so that the final decision is a consensus among group members. In this case, the manager is willing to trade some managerial authority for consensus decisions made by the command group.

The most beneficial aspect of the participative management technique is that it gives subordinates ownership of the decisions of the unit. Individually and collectively, they tend to feel they own whatever decisions are made in the unit. This sense of ownership usually generates commitment to action to realize the objectives of their collective decisions, especially when the democratic approach is used. Commitment to their decisions would normally result in commitment to actions that are likely to produce top-quality outcomes. Other major benefits of this technique are team camaraderie and a feeling of importance. Being solicited for advice and input on management decisions bestows recognition to subordinates that they matter, they are intelligent, and they are well appreciated for their quality of mind.

While the participative technique has positive consequences, it also has some drawbacks that deserve mentioning. Among them is that it takes a much longer time to make decisions than with the autocratic method. While the autocrat can authoritatively make all decisions and command workers to do as they are told, the participative technique involves taking the necessary time to get input from the workers. This means urgent decisions are less likely to be made through this method unless they are anticipated far in advance, and the manager can plan for the participation of the unit well in advance of the due date and the execution of particular decisions.

The participative technique is also resource-intensive. It tends to consume a fair volume of organizational resources, especially time and money that fund the many meetings, testimonies (as in the case of political decisions by Congress), and payments to consultants. Also, while this technique can help in team building and fostering group camaraderie, it can result in disunity, fractures, and grumbling among command group members when some members feel their ideas were disregarded during decision-making. This may produce a feeling of being undermined, jealousy, and anger toward those whose ideas dominate a supposed collective decision.

Another fallout of the participative management technique may be unique to the democratic (rather than the consultative) process. It is very common in the democratic process to have less than a unanimous consensus on an idea when subordinates feel very free and comfortable expressing their views on an issue (Halloran

& Benton, 1987). This is especially true when brainstorming for solutions is encouraged and frequently practiced in a unit. The brainstorming process requires the elimination of some ideas since it is unlikely that every suggestion that is contributed will make the final cut for consideration. And, among the ideas that get to the final stage of consideration, votes may be taken to determine which ideas to implement. In the end, the ideas that are selected may not have a unanimous agreement, thereby leading to the imposition of the accepted ideas of some members over the entire unit. This shows how the democratically designed approach often results in impositions on those with different or opposing views and interests. This indicates that depending on the size of a unit or command group, some people will feel imposed upon by decisions they did not favor. This is an iron cage of unintended consequences of the common democratic process. It is unavoidable in common democracy that the will of some people will be imposed on others. This imposition is what Lani Guinier (1994), a professor at Harvard University, termed *The Tyranny of the Majority*. In her book, which carries the same title as the phrase, Professor Guinier demonstrated how the democratic process as an attempt at practicing equality in decision-making produces the unintended negative consequence of oppressing or tyrannizing others with nondominant voices.

The Laissez-faire Management Technique.

Laissez-faire is a French word that means hands-off. Another term that describes this technique is free rein. As a management technique, it means a manager has a hands-off approach to coordinating the activities and labor of the subordinates. By hands-off, a manager mainly gives instructions about goals to be achieved by individuals and the unit, and she leaves the subordinates alone to figure out how the goals are to be achieved. In some cases, a manager may only give a general idea of objectives and then allow the subordinates to determine goals, processes, and means of achievement by themselves (Halloran & Benton, 1987). This technique is mostly reserved for highly skilled and professional employees who mainly work on projects that require advanced skills and knowledge, independence, and great personal discretion. These workers do not require close supervision and often resent such supervision. In a study of a large corporation in the aerospace industry, it was found that engineers and scientists who experienced directives rather than laissez-faire treatment by their supervisors registered a high level of job alienation and unhappiness (Miller, 1967). The manager who supervises professional workers is well advised to understand and practice laissez-faire for team success.

A manager in a software development corporation may, for example, tell her subordinates that the organization wants their unit to develop a new game software. She may ask the subordinates to determine what type of software is best to create, as well as ask them to design and build it. Each subordinate, in this case, may have to produce a software goal and work to create it according to acceptable organizational bureaucratic protocol. The manager's responsibility to the command group is mainly to support and coordinate. She may be primarily responsible for procuring organizational resources for the team and getting updates from each member to make sure that everyone is on track to meet any milestone goals and finish the final product on time for the organization. The whole process of completing the project will be at the discretion of the workers.

The laissez-faire management technique comes with some major advantages to both organizational members and the organization. It grants respect to employees who are recognized for their knowledge, skills, and self-motivation. Employees who are managed through this method are given plenty of discretionary use of authority to conduct their tasks (Miller, 1967). Such an amount of authority signals to employees that they are trusted to use a high amount of discretionary authority sensibly. It is a signal that the employees would use organizational resources efficiently to meet organizational goals on time. Consequently, laissez-faire encourages employee motivation and the desire to initiate and effectively perform complex assignments (Halloran & Benton, 1987).

While the laissez-faire approach is positive at many levels, as indicated above, it can also be counterproductive to workgroup unity and effective job performance. It has been identified as a major contributor to some organizational dysfunctional behaviors, such as conflicts and aggression (Bass, 1990; Fox & Miles, 2001) and bullying (Leymann, 1996) among co-workers. As explained by Kelloway and colleagues (2005), conditions of conflicts, aggression, abuse, and bullying produce isolation and exclusion among organizational members. These conditions will likely impede group cohesion and erect obstacles against effective job performance at both the individual and workgroup levels. In the end, these dysfunctional consequences signal the greater likelihood that laissez-faire will likely produce weak (rather than strong) interpersonal relations within a workgroup. Given the negative outcomes of the laissez-faire decision approach, its use should be based on a cost-benefit analysis in which its benefits outstrip costs. It may also be used only in conditions in which it is most desirable, such as in supervising professionals whose job requirements include a significant amount of discretionary decision-making.

Bureaucratic Activities and Status

Management is a set of bureaucratic activities that accompany the status of the manager, and the person who occupies the status is expected to perform the duties of the said position. In the context of this book, the manager will mean all levels of management, such as the president, the chief executive officer, vice presidents, managers, and first-line supervisors alike. In essence, anyone who has supervisory duties will be generically referred to as "manager" and performing management duties in this book. In a few instances, the terms manager and supervisor may be used interchangeably in some parts of this book.

Ideally, an organization will have multiple employees who are distributed across the height and breadth of the organizational structure. Along the height of any organizational structure are managerial positions. These positions are built into the structure of an organization as rational-legal (Weber, 1947) to signify their legitimacy. The idea that they are bureaucratically structural means that they are intentionally designed to contribute to the systematic, step-by-step processes through which organizational goals are efficiently realized. This means that management is structured into the bureaucracy of an organization. It is a recognizable official area of organizational hierarchy where specified organizational decisions are designated to occur. Hence, management is an official organizational position, and the occupant of any specific management position is hired to make certain decisions relative to the occupied position for the organization. This is why the position of a manager and management duties should be recognized in bureaucratic terms as officially designed aspects of organizational processes for goal attainment. It is also why management positions are visible in organizational charts and can be advertised and filled when vacant. The recognition of management positions as bureaucratically structured within an organization's chain of command should be kept in mind for contrast with leadership status in a later chapter.

Doing Things Right

Managerial behaviors include doing things right or correctly (Bennis & Nanus, 2007). Each function and principle of management discussed earlier is expected to be designed to allow organizational activities that lead to goal accomplishments to be carried out *properly and correctly*. Things have to be done correctly as designed, and management is tasked with making sure that correctness is achieved. The manager who does things right uses organizational resources in the right proportion at the right time. The manager is expected to know how and when to cross a "t" and dot an "i" and to do so properly.

Doing things right can also be described in terms of the manager following guidelines and performing organizational functions as demanded by formal organizational bureaucracy, such as those stipulated in employee handbooks. For example, managers must make sure that budgets are prepared well and on time. They must interpret job directives from the top correctly and issue accurate instructions to their subordinates. They must conduct unit meetings effectively and efficiently, be prudent in allocating resources and responsibilities to the right subordinates, supervise well, coordinate various unit tasks effectively and efficiently, enforce organizational and unit rules appropriately and consistently, correctly perform employee assessments, give timely feedback, as well as provide an adequate reward for good job performance consistently with the employee-organization contract.

In doing things right, the manager performs the important role of *administering organizational plans* (Bennis, 1989). This is a crucial and central role for all levels of management, including top executives. Every organization operates on plans and designs, which must be administered for an organization to function well, and managers are assigned the responsibility for implementing these plans. This points to another dimension of doing things right: the dimension of *systems maintenance*. It is the job of managers to maintain organizational systems as they are configured

(Bennis, 1989). Managers are responsible for making sure that organizational systems like communication, technology, reward, and change management, among others, function as designed and expected (Bennis, 1989). Therefore, in doing things right, managers implement organizational visions and work to maintain the status quo of organizational realities. Managers keep an organization, its divisions, and its subunits as they are, not as they could or ought to be.

Maintaining the Zone of Indifference

Managers obtain and maintain subordinates' zone of indifference. The term, zone of indifference, describes the extent to which an employee is willing to allow an organization to dictate his actions and performance (Barnard,1938). It represents the range of activities that an employee is willing to accept from the manager and the amount of effort, skills, loyalty, and creativity the employee is willing to apply to meet the manager's expectations without reservations or resistance (Wood, 2013). This is also described as the zone of acceptance (Simon, 1997). That is, an employee is willing to accept being used to perform organizational tasks within a reasonable and acceptable scope that is recognized by both the employee and manager as legitimate. When you take employment with an organization, you sign a contract that stipulates what the organization wants from you, what you can and cannot do, the expected standard of performance required of you, what time you are to report for work each day, how long you are expected to work, how much the organization would pay you, and many more.

By signing a contract, you are permitting the organization to be in charge of your activities during your working hours and to assign reasonable job-related duties to you. You have allowed the organization to control you and to tell you what to do and not do during those hours. The organization will determine where you work, what you do, how much performance is expected of you, the person with whom you work, the person to whom you report, who will assess your work, who gives you feedback, the feedback you get, etc. Allowing the workplace to determine all these things for you during your work hours indicates your willingness to accept things to be dictated to you by the authority of the organization. That is, you are indifferent to the organization having this control over you and your activities. It does not bother you that the organization must make you do certain job duties because you are willing to trade this control of yourself during those hours for the compensation you receive from the organization.

All the things that you do not mind doing for the organization in exchange for your compensation represent your zone of indifference (Barnard, 1938) or acceptance (Simone, 1997). If you take a job with a McDonald's food restaurant, as an example, and your manager tells you to cook 25 hamburgers, fry five pounds of French fries, and bake one big chocolate cake every hour of your eight-hour shift, doing these things will become your zone of indifference or acceptance. You are indifferent to cooking and baking since they are what you have to do for the job that you take. So, the idea that management obtains and maintains an employee's zone of indifference, in this case, will mean that a good manager will use the knowledge of management functions, principles, and techniques to make you cook and bake as required for your position. The manager is able to use her rational-legal authority to control your behavior within the range that you have surrendered yourself to be told what to do and to perform to her satisfaction. Suppose the manager tells you to do certain things that go beyond your willingness to be controlled. In that case, the manager will be violating your zone of indifference, and this may cause you to protest or even leave the organization.

If, in the above example of a McDonald's restaurant, your manager tells you to return to the restaurant every midnight after the restaurant has closed to the public to balance the store's financial accounts for each day, you may protest against this instruction. You may even quit the organization if you are not willing to give the manager such power over you. In this case, you have perceived your manager as violating your zone of indifference. Balancing the store's financial account is not part of your job, and you have a difference to being told to do it. Even if it is part of your job, you may prefer to do it before midnight and, therefore, refuse to obey the manager's instructions to do it so late at night at the risk of being punished or getting fired from the job. It is, therefore, an important aspect of managerial behavior not to violate subordinates' zone of indifference to avoid their refusal to comply with instructions. Instead, managers should learn to issue instructions that fall within employees' zones of indifference. This concept will be further explained within the leadership context in comparison with management in the next chapter.

CHAPTER 5

UNDERSTANDING LEADERSHIP

Followers Determine Their Leaders.

Leaders and followers are Informal Outcomes of Interpersonal Relations.

Leaders Do the Right Thing.

LEADERSHIP IS INFLUENCE

Consider the following comments that were derived from multiple sources by James Gibson and his co-authors:

> "As we enter the second decade of the 21st century, there is a perception that corporate America is running out of good leaders. Regardless of whether this claim is true, leadership is becoming increasingly critical in this era of economic recessions, hyper-competition, shortened product life cycles, and globalization. Companies of all sizes are faced with the question of how to ensure that the future supply of leaders has the right skills, abilities, and strategic vision to achieve success. Ignoring the school of thought that some individuals are born to lead, many firms believe that leadership can be developed in a proactive, systematic fashion" (see Gibson et al., 2012, p.313).

The authors added that many large American corporations across multiple industries (such as Burger King, General Electric, Ford Motors, Walgreens, and Home Depot) have invested heavily in developing leadership skills among their promising employees based on the conviction that leadership is learned and developed, rather than ascribed (Gibson et al., 2012).

Comments in the preceding paragraphs reaffirm my assertions at the beginning of this book about the importance of understanding the distinction among all forms of headships, especially those between management and leadership, which are most likely to be conflated with each other. In the previous chapter, the central characteristics of management were explained to allow a good comparison of management with leadership in this chapter.

In the chapters on management, I discussed the functions, principles, and techniques that the manager must master to coordinate the efforts of others toward goal achievement. Being a manager requires adherence to certain principles and procedures that serve as tools for management success. As an organizational bureaucratic position, management has specified prescribed roles and commensurate authority, which leadership does not have. Leadership does not have a set of techniques, functions, principles, authority, and roles like management. Instead, leadership is only the *influential outcome of human relations*. It is a process of coordinating or guiding the activities of others through the *use of influence* gained through positive human relations with others. As mentioned in Chapter Two, *the reliance on influence to get results is the most defining characteristic of leadership.* Such an influence is the outcome of social relations that begin between managers and their subordinates and end as a relationship between leaders and their followers. It is not an organizationally prescribed authority. Therefore, the manager who wants to become a leader must go beyond relying on position authority, the functions, principles, and techniques of management and relate to subordinates in ways that would make them become followers. Such a manager "will no longer act as a person who holds 'the absolute truth,' making decisions to impose on others, but he has to become a leader to ensure an adequate organizational environment where employees can manifest their abilities and initiative at their best" (Vasilescu, 2019, p.48).

In this chapter, I shall examine twelve important competencies or qualities of leadership. It is possible to increase this list with a few more competencies that distinguish leadership from management, but the twelve that I describe below will sufficiently differentiate between the two forms of headship. Many leadership experts and scholars have popularly mentioned some of the competencies in various forms, so they are sufficient in establishing an accurate framework for understanding leadership and leadership expectations. They also suffice in distinguishing leadership from management. The understanding and practice of these competencies are essential to becoming a leader. They express what leaders do. Hence, any manager who aspires to become a leader is encouraged to understand and acquire these competencies.

LEADERSHIP COMPETENCIES

Informal Status

The first and most distinguishing quality of leadership is that it is an informal status. It is not a bureaucratically structured position like management. That is, unlike management, leadership is not an official position that can be found in an organizational or group structure. This is because leadership is simply *the use of influence with others, the followers, to accomplish goals.* One may not even hold a management position to be a leader. If others voluntarily turn to you for guidance, especially when you have no power to impose sanctions on them, they have made you their leader. They have willingly and voluntarily endorsed you to influence them on how to get things done. In doing so, they are willing to listen to your ideas, implement your suggestions, or even copy how you do things. However, the focus of this book concerns how managers, as officeholders, become leaders, so it is the attainment of the leader status by managers that is discussed in this chapter.

The key point here is that leadership is an *informal status* earned through positive relations with followers. As I explained in Chapter Two, this is an area of consensus in the various definitions of leadership by scholars and other authors. As all definitions of leadership indicate, leadership is not an official position located in an organizational structure, despite the fact that it is common to refer to people as leaders because they hold management positions. Followers are the ones who informally bestow leadership on a manager who has built the necessary relationship with them to get their endorsement to use influence rather than managerial authority to coordinate their work. Hence, the manager should not be automatically perceived or titled as a leader. This is, perhaps, the most difficult aspect of leadership for many people to understand and accept because of the common conflation of management with leadership that I discussed in Chapters One and Two. Leadership, as a concept or idea, is mostly misused as a *commonly accepted standard error* (CASE), as I explained in Chapter Two. The misuse of the leadership concept has been ingrained in the minds of the public, workers, and academics alike. We automatically, as an error, refer to people in high administrative or management positions as leaders rather than by their true official positions. The manager is best recognized as a manager because that is the title of the position the person occupies. The same is true for all corporate executives, including the chief executive officer (CEO) and the corporate president. They are not leaders if others only obediently comply with their authority as dictated by an organizational chain of command and bureaucracy.

Job advertisements typically specify management or administrative positions to be filled. A job advertisement caption may say: "Manager Wanted," "Third-Shift Supervisor Wanted," "Vacancy for the Position of Corporate President to be Filled," "Athletic Director Needed," or "Head Coach Wanted." Job advertisements usually do not say "Leader Wanted" when trying to hire a manager. And, on any occasions that such advertisements exist, the term, leader is used in error. A head coach can be hired, but only the players will decide if the coach is their leader or not. Being a coach does not automatically ordain someone as a leader. Leadership has to be earned from the players, but the hiring organization can put an individual in the position of coach regardless of the opinions of the players about the person. Simply put, a leader cannot be hired because it is not a formal organizational status. *A leader cannot be hired because leadership is based on one's quality of human relations, which induces others to grant someone the privilege to influence them.* Unless one becomes a leader through human relations, one cannot influence others to work. Hence, only managers of any level can be hired, but not a relationship or an influence. Leadership should always be recognized as an *informal source of influence* that is used to inspire or motivate the actions of others. It is an error to see it as a bureaucratic position, and this error should be avoided.

Not too long ago, I delivered a leadership workshop at a professional conference of applied academic and non-academic professionals. One of the attendees at my workshop took an aversion to the concept that managers were not leaders merely by virtue of their positions. She believed that managers, especially top-level executives, were organizational leaders. She spoke of them as "our leadership team" in her organization. I asked why they were not just her organization's top management, executive, upper management, or administrative team. This is because it is correct that managers or administrators in an organization collectively constitute a management or administrative group rather than a leadership group. The characterization of management groups as leadership groups is another common misnomer and CASE. Unless it is a known fact that a manager has become a leader by virtue of being followed by at least one person, what is known as a fact is that a collective of managers is a management group. As stated in one source:

> Management as a group refers to all those persons who perform the tasks of managing an enterprise. When we say that the management of ABC Company is good, we are referring to a group of people who are managing the company. Thus, as a group, technically speaking, management will include all managers, from the chief executive to the first-line managers (lower-

level managers). But in common practice, reference to management tends to imply only top management, i.e., Chief Executive Officer, Chairman, General Manager, Board of Directors, etc. In other words, management tends to be applied to those who make important decisions, who enjoy the authority to allocate resources, and who have responsibility for the efficient utilization of resources to efficiently accomplish organizational objectives. Managers as a group may be perceived in two different ways: all managers taken together, regardless of level of management, or just top managers (Management Basics, 2024, online).

I explained to the workshop participant that her executives might have been leaders to some people in the organization, but it was also possible they were not leaders to anyone. However, what was known about them, without question, was that they were managers and executives; hence, it was best to describe them correctly as top management, executive, or administrative groups. It is important to avoid conflating management and leadership, as I explained in the earlier chapters of this book. But, being welded to the conflation, my workshop participant displayed some dissatisfaction and uneasiness at my distinction between management and leadership groups. She appeared to be unsettled with the distinctions, which were new and contradictory to her established institutionalized view of leadership. My explanation was unsettling to her, perhaps because it violated her perceptions of her top executives. She indicated that she preferred to describe her executive group as her leadership team because of her conventional perception of high-level executives as organizational leaders. She came to the workshop with the perception that leadership was organizationally ordained, like management, and her attachment to that common misnomer (CASE) made it difficult for her to understand leadership with a different but accurate meaning. To see leadership purely as a relational influence rather than a bureaucratic position was difficult for this attendee. I assume this difficulty is reasonably common with most people in organizations.

When both academic and professional business authors conflate management with leadership on a regular basis, it is only sensible to expect the average (non-academic) manager or supervisor to also conflate the two concepts and to do so with emotional convictions. It may, however, also be true that the conference attendee was already a follower of one or more executives in her corporation and, therefore, perceived them as leaders. If this were true, she would be justified in proclaiming her executives as her leaders. But, even in such a situation, the executives may not be leaders to other workers, and it would still have been more accurate for her to describe them as her leaders rather than leaders to the entire organizational membership. Eventually, after a healthy involvement of other workshop participants in the discussion, the attendee in question finally understood leadership as an influencing behavior rather than a synonym for an executive.

Goal Attainment

The leadership competence of goal attainment is shared with management. Leadership is purposeful and goal-oriented; therefore, the ultimate outcome of a leader's behavior is to accomplish organizational goals. In a simple way, *the essence of leadership* is *the use of influence by one person to guide another or others toward the attainment of an objective* (Rodrigues, 2001). This is an important characteristic that affirms that leadership is for goal attainment, just like management. Both are intended to produce organizational success. But, recognizing that leadership is only an informal status of workplace influence, *leadership itself is not and cannot be assigned any goal to achieve.* Instead, management is the official status to which the attainment of any organizational goal is assigned. Therefore, the manager is the person who has the responsibility to achieve organizational (that is, managerial) goals. So, in reality, *the goals that are accomplished through leadership are management goals.* Therefore, leadership can be more accurately defined as *the influencing process of accomplishing managerial goals,* and the leader is the manager who has developed the level of relationship that grants influence as the main tool of goal attainment rather than managerial authority.

An additional aspect of the purpose of leadership is that it is also a process of inspiring others to want to participate in goal attainment. While it does happen that workers who are uninspired and unhappy with their jobs may ritualistically meet their goal objectives in exchange for their income, such a situation does not promote employee motivation or commitment to the organization. At best, such a situation will promote continual commitment whereby the worker remains with an organization until a better job is obtained (Mayer & Allen, 1991; Oyinlade & Christo, 2020). Through leadership, workers gain meaning and interest in collective goals. According to William Pride and his colleagues, *leadership is motivating* because it provides reasons for others to want to work for collective goals in the interests of their organizations (Pride et al., 2008). This means leadership is internally energizing and encouraging. This motivational dimension of leadership is important. It indicates that a leader behaves in ways that create motivating environments and conditions in which the internal energies of others are released in the interests of collective goals. To do this, leadership attainment requires achieving expressive goals in addition to the instrumental ones.

As explained in the last chapter, managers are expected to achieve instrumental goals that are assigned to their positions. They are evaluated and rewarded only for achieving instrumental goals. Hence, they use management techniques and rely on the authority of their positions to achieve their goals. Since they are not held accountable for expressive goals, these goals are typically not of high priority to them. This is a major distinction between managers and leaders. Because leaders rely purely on the use of influence, which is derived from building positive relationships with workers, *achieving expressive goals is highly important for being a leader*. When the expressive needs of workers are met, they are likely to be happy to be part of their workgroup and achieve solidarity with their coworkers. While expressive goals are extrinsic rather than intrinsic job factors that are responsible for motivation, achieving them eliminates or significantly reduces dissatisfaction with their manager and workgroup. This means that to be a leader, a manager must actively accomplish both instrumental and expressive goals.

Influence Through Endorsed Power

By now, it has been fully established that leadership relies on influence rather than position or bureaucratic authority in coordinating and guiding the work of others toward goal accomplishments. In the leadership context, influence can be described as a non-coercive variant of power that relies on the use of *inspirational appeal* and *rational persuasion* to get results in specific situations at specific times (see Oyinlade et al., 2003). Inspirational appeal describes the ability to create excitement and enthusiasm and arouse positive emotions in others, while rational persuasion is the use of logic and factual evidence to generate convictions (Yukl et al., 1992). This supports the idea that *leadership is about influencing others without force, coercion, threat of punishment, or promise of reward* (Katz & Kahn, 1978). This does not mean that a leader does not or cannot reward others. The point is that people are influenced by the leader, not for the sake of getting a particular reward or fear of getting punished (Katz & Kahn, 1978). It means the leader influences others' behaviors based on a willing endorsement of the leader to exert influence that others would accept. This is the point of *endorsed power*.

Endorsed power is significantly different from authorized power, which characterizes management. The *authorized power* of the manager is not personal. The power belongs to the organization rather than the person of the manager. It is the authority embedded in the position occupied, and the manager uses it to get work done (Weber,1947). Endorsed power, however, belongs to the followers, and it is given to the leader as a person rather than to the office that is occupied in the organization (Dornbusch & Scott, 1975). Endorsed power is voluntarily given to the leader by the followers who have accepted an individual as their leader. It is the followers who determine the legitimacy of the leader's instructions and the extent to which they would be followed in a bottom-up power dynamic (Barnard, 1938).

The concept of endorsed power will be used with a slight modification from its original description by Chester Barnard (1938) and its use by Sanford Dornbusch and W. Richard Scott (1975). These earlier descriptions conceptualized endorsed power mainly as a legitimization of managerial authority. For example, Chester Barnard explained that if workers refuse to acknowledge authority by refusing to obey, the authority giver cannot be said to have authority over the workers. It is, therefore, the willingness of the workers to obey authority that confers authority on the manager. This claim by Barnard can be easily challenged and defeated by the fact that managerial instructions are based on authorized power, which subordinates are compelled to obey, unless in cases of insurgency. Because endorsed power is being used here as a leadership condition, I use it with a slight modification from its original use.

As a leadership condition, endorsed power is used in this book consistently with the description of influence described by Amitai Etzioni (1965) to mean *the willingness of others to allow someone to convince them to willingly align their interests with those of the person.* Followers entrust the leader with the privilege to influence them according to the wishes of the leader. Through their endorsement, followers are willing to accept directives from the leader because they voluntarily wish to go along with the leader's choices (Katz & Kahn, 1978). Endorsed power, therefore, as used in this book to represent leadership influence, is synonymous with *bestowed privilege* or *power.* It is power given by the bottom (followers) to the top (leader).

An important distinction to recognize is that the word, power, in endorsed power does not mean the same thing as in the use of authoritarian power and managerial authority that contain coercive properties. In endorsed power, the properties of power are limited to the non-coercive influence of the leader. Unlike authorized power that can be withdrawn by an organization, either by eliminating a manager through dismissal from office, redesigning a management position, or completely eliminating it, only the followers who bestowed endorsed power can withdraw it because it is bottom-up. This is grounded in the position of Meindl and colleagues (1985), who state that leadership is bestowed on someone by followers. Therefore, when followers withdraw endorsed power, a leader is transformed back into a manager, and the followers also revert to being subordinates.

The extent of endorsed power given to a leader determines the extent to which the leader can influence followers. So, the person who is given a great amount of endorsed power can influence others with greater intensity over a wide range of goals than someone given minimum endorsed power. It, therefore, follows that the expansiveness of bestowed endorsed power can be a measure of leadership status. The greater the expansiveness of bestowed endorsed power and the larger the number of workers that grant it, the greater the status of the leader to the followers. Hence, a great leader will be someone who is given a great amount of endorsed power by the vast majority of the people who report to the person. Being granted a great amount of endorsed power by many people will also mean a great ability for high achievements due to the willingness of followers to perform beyond expectations. The high accomplishments under the leader add to the greatness of the leader as well as affirm it.

We may ask what determines the endorsement of someone for leadership. The answer lies in group characteristics, such as what is important to a group. The endorsement of someone for leadership is not a static concept but one that is deeply influenced by the context of the group. For instance, a criminal gang that is regularly embroiled in fights with rival gangs and also frequently clashes with the police may prioritize boldness and the ability to unite members as the most important criteria for becoming a leader. In such a scenario, the gang is likely to bestow endorsed power on a member who displays the qualities of boldness and camaraderie, which are crucial for facing common enemies.

It may also be the case that the person who commands great charisma in the eyes of group members is the person who is endorsed with the power of influence. What is charisma? Charisma describes personal qualities that others find attractive, compelling, respected, and admirable (Hughes et al.,1999). Charisma is about the qualities of an individual that others admire and may even wish to emulate. Aristotle's popular ideas of ethos, pathos, and logos are useful in identifying three aspects of charisma that may result in the conferral of leadership on a manager.

A manager who exhibits *ethos* demonstrates ethical or moral character. Ethos includes reliability, credibility, and trustworthiness in an individual, while *pathos* is the ability to move others emotionally. Lastly, *logos* is the use of intellect to give others good, logical, factual, and compelling reasons for action (McCormack, 2014; Mshvenieradze, 2013). The combination of ethos, pathos, and logos will enhance one's ability to persuade others and, therefore, serve as an important basis for conferring endorsed power on a manager. It will be easy to grant endorsed power to a manager who is believed to have ethical and moral character, who can connect with workers emotionally, and who also uses facts and logic, rather than position power, to encourage others to work.

Followership

Followership is defined here as the alignment of one's thoughts, preferences, and actions with those of another person, the leader, based on high regard and affective reverence for the person and without any inducement or expectations of rewards or threat of punishment. Followership is a past or current action, but it is not an intent or desire for a future action. It describes one's past or current relationship with another person. I derived this definition from all that I have explained and discussed so far about management, leadership, power, authority, as well as authorized and endorsed power. It is synthesized from all relevant analyses, explanations, and discussions of both management and leadership up to this point. As mentioned earlier, leadership involves the use of non-coercive influence and the absence of authorized power granted by an organization. If someone behaves as you instructed, for a certain benefit or reward, or out of fear of punishment, the person is not your follower but your subordinate. This is an important reason the manager has subordinates, but the leader has followers. Followership is not the action of subordinates. It is the action of followers.

Just as it is important not to conflate or equate management with leadership, the same is true of subordinates and followers. The subordinate has no choice but to obey and comply. Subordination is not up to the subordinate to choose when to be or not be one unless, of course, one leaves an organization. It is also not up to the subordinate to choose the manager, except in cases where a chairperson is elected or appointed by the votes of the subordinates, as may occur at corporate board levels and advanced professional units of professional organizations like the university and large law firms. It is, therefore, the case that in management, a manager is the manager of all command group members. Regardless of how everyone in a command group may feel, they are all subordinates to the authority of the manager, whether they like it or not, so long as they remain in the workgroup under the manager.

Unlike management, leadership does not grant universal influence over an entire command group. Because leadership is based on the voluntary bestowing of endorsed power of influence on a manager, only those who willingly and voluntarily confer endorsed power on the manager become followers as they turn the manager into their leader. One does not become a leader until someone decides to follow willingly and voluntarily. While it is the manager's relations and actions toward the subordinates that transform them into followers, it is not until followership occurs that the manager becomes a leader. This is a reciprocal relationship between a leader and a follower. The two develop as a role-set through reciprocity of goodwill ferried through human relations. It also means that, unlike management, which grants the manager authority over everyone in a command group, a manager becomes a leader only to those who choose to follow rather than to everyone in the command group. Therefore, a position holder, such as a manager or senior executive, cannot command subordinates to become followers. Unlike being a subordinate, being a follower is a willing and voluntary affective (sentimental) response to a manager who is being made a leader. By having affective feelings for a leader, followers display a likeness, respect, and admiration for the person. They hold the leader in high regard and reverence. When a manager becomes a leader, she gains followers from her subordinates and enjoys the benefits of their affective feelings. This culminates in receiving endorsed power and the ability to use influence rather than managerial authority to accomplish managerial goals.

Another important fact about leadership is relevant at this point. Leadership is mostly implicitly declared or stated. It is subtly demonstrated through the actions of followers. It is the unspoken, informal consequences of behaviors and relationships with subordinates. Leadership is recognized when subordinates willingly act as followers. I will share a personal experience to illustrate how managers can inferentially recognize they have become leaders through the actions of their followers.

I used to coach a soccer club named the Star City Rangers in the Lincoln Adult Soccer Association League, an amateur soccer league in Lincoln, Nebraska, from the 1990s through the early 2000s. The games in the league were played on Saturdays and Sundays. At the end of one of our games, I spoke to the team about the following week's game against one of my team's top rivals. I indicated that I wanted every player to show up for the next weekly practice and be present for the following week's game on Saturday. One of my players, a midfielder whom I shall call Josh, as a pseudonym to protect his privacy, pulled me to the side and informed me that he would not be able to attend the following week's game because he had to be at an important wedding in Denver that Saturday. The distance between Lincoln and Denver was approximately 450 miles, and it would take roughly seven hours to drive. The time of the wedding was around noon, and my team's game was to start at six o'clock that mid-September day. There was no way Josh could return to Lincoln on time for the game after the wedding. He apologized to me for his intended absence at an important game, and I told him not to worry or feel guilty. Although he was the best on the team for his position, I had other players who could substitute for him. I wished him a safe trip and a good time at the wedding.

The following Saturday arrived, and, as usual, my players arrived 45 minutes early to dress up and participate in our usual warm-up drills before the start of any game. About 15 minutes before the game started, I rallied the team together to tell them about the format we were going to play that day and showed each of the eleven starters their respective positions. In the middle of my instruction, one of my players said: "Coach, we have another player coming…. it is Josh!" I looked up, and there he was, Josh, running across the field to our huddle. He told me he was ready for the game, but he was still wearing the tuxedo he wore for the wedding. He quickly changed into the team's uniform, warmed up, and I put him in the game. We won the game! As the team was about to depart after the game had ended, I pulled Josh to the side to thank him for coming to the game, and I asked him if he got a speeding ticket on his return trip to Lincoln. I estimated that he could only have arrived on time for the game by driving at a ridiculously fast speed that could have earned him a speeding ticket or even a night in a police jail if the highway patrol officers had caught him speeding excessively. But what he said surprised me. He said he bought an expensive one-way ticket to fly back to Lincoln after the wedding, and he arranged for someone to pick him up at the airport and drive him straight to the game. I was shocked and told him he should not have paid so much money just to make it back in time for a game in a city league.

More surprising was that Josh did not attend the wedding reception, and he left his travel companions in Denver. He also told me that he saw the reaction on my face when he informed me that he would not be able to attend the game, and he thought he had disappointed me. He said my body language showed I was not happy that he would miss a big game, despite my attempts to conceal my letdown and my wishing him a great time at the wedding. So, he did everything he could to be at the game, including spending plenty of money on a one-way flight ticket just so that he would not disappoint me. I profusely expressed my gratitude for the honor he bestowed on me with his actions. It was at this time that I realized that to Josh, I was beyond a coach and a teammate. I was a leader to him. While I might have only been the team's coach and teammate to other players, Josh made me recognize I was a leader to him by inference from his actions. He allowed me to influence him without any inducement of reward for playing or threat of punishment for not playing a game. When a subordinate responds to a manager in such a way as to be willing to perform beyond expectations only for the sake of affective relations, the manager has succeeded in transforming the particular subordinate into a follower. The worker is no longer a subordinate.

It is important to note that if managers are to become leaders, they must first transform their subordinates into followers by earning their endorsement for influence. Converting subordinates into followers is the very first step in becoming a leader. Without converting any subordinate into a follower, one remains only a manager, regardless of how good a manager one may be. This fact points to the reality of being a leader as the co-creation of both the leader and the followers. It is when the manager is able to convert subordinates into followers that he is ordained as a leader. Hence, the emergence of a leader is co-created by the leader and his followers (Uhl-Bien et al., 2014). So, both leader and follower occupy the same relationship space where they mutually determine the existence of each other (Koveshnikov, 2022). It also follows that the extent to which one is a leader depends on the number of subordinates who have converted into followers. Hence, the leader to one follower may only be a manager to another worker within the same workgroup. This means being a leader does not eradicate being a manager. Both statuses may simultaneously co-exist in one person. This accords the manager two possible sets of power: bureaucratic managerial authority (i.e., authorized power) and influence (i.e., endorsed power) bestowed by followers. At this juncture, it is important to discuss the role of perceptions in what constitutes influence through endorsed power and what constitutes bureaucratic authority.

Perceptions and Relativity of Managerial Authority.

Managers, by virtue of their positions, are accorded bureaucratic authority, which subordinates must accept and obey. Compliance with managerial authority is expected as a standard behavior from subordinates. At the same time, a manager may be given endorsed power of influence by the subordinates who have become his followers and perceive him as their leader. The question, now, is, what type of power are subordinates responding to when the manager issues a directive? Are subordinates responding to a managerial authority or to an informal leadership influence through endorsed power? The answer to this question will demonstrate the complication of becoming a leader while simultaneously holding a management position.

The answer can be obtained by inquiring about the basis of responses to managerial actions. When workers respond by obedience and keep their preferences in abeyance, they react as subordinates to the group head as a manager. However, when they respond out of affection by altering and aligning their preferences with those of the group head, they react as followers to a leader (Etzioni, 1965).

The exercise of authority or use of influence is, therefore, subject to relative interpretation by subordinates. It also means that only the subordinates can determine who they follow based on how they interpret their relationships with their manager. They are the only ones who can make a manager a leader based on their individual decisions to become followers as a result of their individual relations with the manager. However, the interpretation of manager-subordinate interpersonal relations does not emerge from thin air. All previous interactions and experiences with the manager shape it.

All interactions serve as input that forms the basis for how the actions and instructions of a manager are interpreted as a power move. Hence, what one worker (a subordinate) may interpret as the use of an authority that must be obeyed, another worker (a follower) may perceive only as an influence that is reciprocated with an affectionate willingness to perform.

Lastly, you may ask yourself if you are a follower of someone. What patterns in your behavior make you a follower? If you are willing to perform beyond normal job expectations, mainly to make a particular person look good, if you affectively look up to a particular person for guidance, if you trust the judgments of a particular person as always good and fair, if you ask yourself what a particular person would do in a particular situation so that you could do the same thing, if you like being around a particular person at and away from your workplace, if you enjoy doing non-job-related things for a particular person, if you eagerly go to work every day because you look forward to interacting with a particular person, if you eagerly take instructions from a particular person, and if all these things apply to you without any inducement of, or expectations for, reward or threat of punishment, you are a follower of that particular person. As evident in the characteristics of followership, the criteria for followership are much higher than for being a subordinate, which only requires occupying a position that reports to a manager and obeying the manager's instructions for rewards or avoiding punishments. Because the requirements for followership are high, I dub being a follower the highest form of flattery, respect, trust, and regard one human being has for another.

Doing the Right Thing

As expressed by Warren Bennis, "...to survive in the twenty-first century, we are going to need a new generation of leaders—leaders, *not* managers. The distinction is an important one. Leaders conquer the context—the volatile, turbulent, ambiguous surroundings that sometimes seem to conspire against us and will surely suffocate us if we let them—while managers surrender to it" (Bennis, 1989, p. 7). In that comment, Bennis pointed to the importance of leadership over management in handling difficult situations. As explained in Chapter Four, managers specialize in doing things right or correctly. That is what Bennis referred to as surrendering to a suffocating context in the above statement.

The idea of surrendering to the context implies that a manager, especially a good one, works within the suffocating conditions (the status quo conditions) of work to meet expectations. This is not necessarily a bad thing or an indictment for wrongdoing by managers. Instead, it acknowledges the skill and ability of managers to still meet job expectations despite difficulties in the job environment. However, while a manager does things right and meets outcome expectations within prevailing suffocating contexts, a leader takes the difficult action of rectifying the situation by changing the context to be non-suffocating. This is a major difference between a manager and a leader, which Bennis addressed in that statement. As Bennis also later coined, the leader does the right thing (Bennis & Nanus, 2007). Doing the right thing is what leaders do, even when it is a challenging ordeal, unpopular, and may cause a rebuke. It may not be as easy as one may prefer. Many managers may say they strive to always do the right thing, but striving is different from doing it. To strive or to try is to allow oneself plenty of room to fall short of doing the right thing and, therefore, not be able to make the transition from management to leadership.

When it comes to doing the right thing, most people only "talk the talk," but a leader walks the talk. Doing the right thing is a conscious decision, not a wish or a desire. "A decision is a commitment – a resolution to do or stop doing an act or to adopt or reject an attitude" (Benton, 1998, p. 422). When a person has made a decision, he has "(1) started a series of behavioral reactions in favor of something, or it may mean (2) that he has made up his mind to do a certain action, which he has no doubts that he ought to do. But perhaps the most common use of the term is this: 'to make a decision' means (3) to make a judgment regarding what one ought to do in a certain situation after having deliberated on some alternative courses of action" (Ofstad, 1961, p. 15). Therefore, doing the right thing as a leadership behavior should not be perceived as a philosophy or an ideology but as an action, and it is one that I recommend should be practiced as a principle to ensure consistency and permanence.

We may ask the question, what constitutes the right thing to do? When is an action the proper one? A good answer is that a behavior is the right thing to do when it is consistent with a rational person's view of what is fair, necessary, non-biased, reasonable, deserved, or justified within a particular context. A rational or sensible person should be able to observe the actions of a manager and affirm them as the right thing to do based on the relative context in which the manager must act. The social context in which an action takes place is important in deciding what the right thing is and if the right thing has been done. Hence, the right thing should be considered as a relative judgment. What is right in one situation in one organization may not necessarily be right in a different context and a different organization. It is, therefore, important to understand the conditions or factors that may affect whether or not the right thing is done. To this effect, the following section will review some factors that contribute to doing the right thing.

Factors that Affect Doing the Right Thing

To start, we may ask why doing the right thing is a domain of leadership while managers are expected to only do things right. That is, why do some managers only do things right while others go beyond it and also do the right thing, which is a leadership behavior? Why do all managers not do the right thing and gain leadership quality? These questions indicate that a leader simultaneously occupies a management position, performs managerial functions, and adheres to management principles. This fact reveals another understanding of the nature of leadership as a relational method for accomplishing managerial goals through the use of influence. *Leadership is a method of using influence rather than managerial techniques and authority to achieve management goals since management is the official position in an organizational structure to which official goals are assigned.* If some managers do things right but others also do the right thing, what factors shape which of the two a manager does? While many factors may shape the option between doing things right and doing the right thing, good decision-making, management training, and courage are three important factors that will be discussed here. But, in order to fully elaborate on courage, it will be addressed as a leadership competence separately from the other two factors.

Making Good Decisions. For a manager to transcend doing things right and instead do the right thing, she must have the skills and competency to use discretion to consistently make good decisions. Doing the right thing inherently implies knowing what is right and doing it. But what is a good decision? In the most basic sense, a good decision is a judgment about options and actions that solve a problem or advance a change based on a well-calculated cost-benefit analysis. It is a judgment about actions being embarked upon, perhaps among other alternatives, which produce the best-desired outcomes with the least undesirable consequences, given the particular set of circumstances in which the decision is being made.

A good decision will comprise at least three types of judgments: *technical, value,* and *practical.* These components are adapted from the works of Marcia Angell (1999), Richard Dow (1999), and Amanda Ratliff (1999) on good decisions in the medical environment. A ***technical Judgment*** refers to the derivation of technical answers for technical questions concerning specific technical problems facing an organization. It includes answers to how the problem is to be diagnosed, how to collect and analyze appropriate data, how to examine potential benefits and risks of alternative solutions, and how to assess the ramifications of not choosing particular options (Angell, 1999; Ratliff, 1999).

Because this decision is technical, it should be made only by organizational officials who have specialized technical skills. These persons should be skilled at analyzing both quantitative and qualitative data (Angell, 1999) and should make decisions without bias, such as the *last case bias* (Ratliff, 1999) or the recency bias of how the problems that were recently solved shape how a new problem is being solved.

Value judgment (Angell, 1999; Ratliff, 1999) is adapted here to mean the extent to which decisions are consistent with the standards of right and wrong of an entity. It is a measure of compatibility between a decision and an entity's values (Dow, 1999). The entity may be an organization, a unit, or a manager. These standards may be part of an organization's ethical considerations for acceptable behaviors. This means that a leader weighs decisions against an organization's standards of acceptable actions to solve particular problems. Because of such consideration, a value judgment may prevent a decision from being made if the decision opposes the values (especially the core ones) of an organization. This may be the case in situations where a cost-effective solution may have foreseeable detrimental consequences to an organization's values relative to its community, customers, or other organizational stakeholders. By weighing the foreseeable outcomes of a decision against the values of an organization, managers may opt for a less-than-optimum (that is, sufficing) action to avoid violating organizational values and potential negative consequences from such a violation.

A *practical Judgement* is the likelihood that a decision is workable, rational, or functional (Dow, 1999). It indicates that a decision about the right thing to do must be doable and will solve the problem at hand. This component is crucial for doing the right thing because the right thing must be implemented to translate into leadership quality. It informs the decision-maker that just because a solution appears to be cost-effective and meets organizational value standards does not mean it can be implemented in light of insurmountable obstacles within and from outside of the organization. Obstacles may include "elements—such as affordability, efficacy, complexity, availability of appropriate support systems, geography, transportation, and many other factors (Dow, 1999, p. 187)." So, in the end, organizational solutions require workable and practicable decisions that are assessed relative to their particular organizational environment at a given time.

Management Training. Management training prepares managers to provide the means for achieving the goals (or ends) assigned to their specific positions in their organizational structure. Keep in mind that these goals are assigned to the position of management; hence, anyone (manager) who occupies the position becomes the one responsible for achieving the goals. To achieve their assigned goals, managers use existing established methods and resources available to them in their organization. However, by using already established protocols, they become limited in their abilities to perceive alternative courses of action. This is a condition of trained incapacity (Veblen, 2019) in which managers are so well-trained to perform their duties that they become incompetent in seeing other perspectives that might be necessary for doing the right thing. When managers focus on meeting their assigned goals by conventional methods, their devotion to mechanical protocols often results in an analytic blind spot. This prevents them from evaluating what they are doing and recognizing alternative courses of action that could be more effective and efficient than the accustomed convention. As Bennis may put it, they confine themselves to working within suffocating conditions rather than changing the conditions (see Bennis, 1989). Therefore, doing things right rather than doing the right thing is mostly the consequence of managerial training and expectations. This phenomenon was captured in Robert K. Merton's (1968) book on *Social Structures and Social Theories,* in which he discussed John Dewey's concept of Occupational Psychosis and Daniel Warnotte's Professional Deformation. Both conditions capture related but different dimensions of trained incapacity.

Occupational psychosis describes a manager's mindset of a rigid bureaucratic pattern of behavior in meeting role objectives (see Merton, 1968). The manager who demonstrates occupational psychosis is committed to a rigid, conventional pattern of role performance and rejects any new way of reasoning. Such a person will not entertain other possible and potentially more efficient ways of completing tasks and accomplishing goals. The person is a master of bureaucratic steps in work processes and rigidly adheres to the steps like an automatic machine without missing a bit. This strict attachment to the familiar conventional methods produces the inability to consider and, therefore, rejects alternative steps that may be more effective or efficient than the conventional ones.

Professional deformation, similar to occupational psychosis, describes the condition in which a manager sees reality only from her professional training and role expectations such that she becomes resistant to any other disciplinary perspective (Isonen, 2016; Merton, 1968). It is a deformation in that by performing consistently with rigidity from a professional educational perspective and job expectations, the manager acts only according to these standards and is unable to divorce herself from them to take a course of action outside the ingrained professional standards. This may be observed when a manager focuses exclusively on how to accomplish a goal strictly by the standards of her profession alone. She overlooks why the goal ought to be achieved, what outcomes are expected, what outcomes could be achieved, and the right way to accomplish the best results. If the prevailing organizational conditions are suffocating, a leader will make the right decision (i.e., do the right thing). Such decisions often require mixing different but legitimate methods from multiple disciplinary perspectives. In some cases, such decisions may also contradict executive directives to accomplish certain outcomes. In sum, if a manager has reasons to contradict executive directives or conventional disciplinary methods as the right thing to do in a particular context, she should do so to achieve the best outcome and avoid being a victim of professional deformation.

The theme in these three concepts (trained incapacity, occupational psychosis, and professional deformation) is that organizational bureaucracy unintentionally imposes challenges that hinder the abilities of managers to become leaders. Organizational bureaucracy prescribes a series of actions to be taken to achieve a unit's goals. It determines what is to be done, how it should be done, and the division of labor for getting it done. It determines what skills are developed and are not developed, what is encouraged and what is not encouraged, as well as what is noticed and what is not noticed. It dictates the means-to-end behavior of a manager, and it prevents the manager from engaging in behaviors outside the means-to-end relationship. While organizational bureaucratic objectives may include the development of managers for leadership, the same bureaucracy forces the manager to a busy routine of doing things right by providing means to achieve goals through conventional methods. The adherence to means-to-end traditional protocols prevents the manager from questioning the status quo, which may elicit doing the right thing by deviating from conventional ways to pursue a perceived right course of action. This shows how organizational bureaucracy may impose limitations on the ability of managers to gain the leadership quality of doing the right thing. This is an internal contradiction of organizational bureaucracy, which is often unrecognized, and which becomes a roadblock for managers to become leaders. Managers are forced to play it safe by following conventional organizational protocols; hence, they do things right. Or, they may do the right thing and risk violating professional standards and conventional protocols at the expense of personal convenience and likely punishment. This signifies why becoming a leader and remaining one requires immense courage.

Courage

As mentioned in the preceding section, leadership requires doing the right thing, and this may happen at the expense of personal inconvenience and, or with the likelihood of punishments, which may include getting laid off. Therefore, becoming a leader requires having the courage to make tough, sometimes politically incorrect, and punishable decisions. It means that to be a leader is to have courage! It is to have the courage to say "yes" when "yes" must be said and to say "no" when "no" is appropriate. As an elementary school pupil in Nigeria during the 1970s, I learned a song that was popularly taught to elementary school children in the country. The lyrics to the song were:

> "Wherever you go,
> Wherever you are,
> Do not say yes,
> When you mean to say no."

As I reflect in hindsight, this song taught me a lesson in courage. It informed my young mind, like those of other children, of the virtue of courage. It taught us not to be afraid, and if we were afraid, not to be paralyzed with fear. We should be courageous in asserting our positions. Essentially, the song taught us to be courageous in doing the right thing in the face of any difficulty and possible punishment.

We can consider courage as a major factor that affects the likelihood that a manager would do the right thing instead of just doing things right. Doing the right thing is often difficult, especially in today's organizational environments that seem to push organizational officers to make sentimental decisions rather than purely rational decisions in the best interests of effectiveness and efficiency. Rational decisions that are best for an organization often require great courage in the face of restrictive external and internal special interest pressures. These pressures demand that organizational decision-makers make decisions that favor various organizational constituents rather than decisions that are best for organizational survival and organizational members as a whole.

An external organizational environment often includes various advocacy groups that pressure organizations to adopt new policies that favor various interest groups or populations. These advocacy groups may demand that organizational officers grant various concessions under the virtues of diversity, equity, accessibility, and inclusion for various population categories, such as racial, ethnic, gender, religious, disabilities, and sexual identities, in the United States and Western countries. Government policies and political trends such as affirmative action, diversity programs, safe space, social justice, corporate social responsibility, environmental, social, and governance (ESG) forces, etc., may also pressure organizational managers to make less-than-optimum cost-saving and revenue-generating decisions. An organization's internal environment may also foster trends and patterns of societally acceptable philosophies and ideologies rather than what is best for the organization. This is especially common in literacy organizations, like the news media and academic organizations, where decision-makers tend to support organizational actions that are consistent with social trends. For example, it is fast becoming commonplace to assault free speech and academic freedom in these organizations with the blessings of their top officials who lack the courage to openly protect free speech and academic freedom.

Workers' unions may also launch internal pressures to compel senior managers and executives to take measures to do things that benefit workers or coalitions of workers, at a potential detriment to the organization. How well a senior-level decision-maker is able to make the right decision for the well-being of the organization and its entire constituencies depends on the extent to which courage is displayed against union pressures. Also, organizational culture provides a structure of tradition and customs into which organizational members, especially those with long tenure, are socialized and through which their daily activities are conducted.

Customs and traditions provide organizational members with stable frameworks for their formal and informal actions, including how to consistently solve problems. An attempt to implement a decision that is not consistent with the current organizational status quo of norms, customs, and traditions will likely ruffle the feathers of many organizational members, especially of those with long-term tenure who have become accustomed and well-adjusted to organizational traditions. For rational decisions to be made with the likelihood that traditional patterns of behaviors would be disrupted, courage is required from decision-makers.

This discussion reveals how the capacity to make tough decisions to do the right thing, especially those that involve unpopular actions, requires courage. It takes courage to make decisions and take actions that will be unpopular with upper management, colleagues, and other workers. This is one reason courage is mostly associated with leadership rather than management. So long as managers find "the how" for completing an assignment, they will fulfill management expectations. But leadership asks the questions, "why" and "why not," which take courage in the face of organizational cultural conservatism and well-established bureaucratic patterns.

Demonstrating courage to make difficult and unpopular decisions can also be difficult for managers because people typically look out for themselves and try to avert what they may lose if they put their neck on the line for someone and the line breaks. This makes it easy for fear to rule the minds of managers, thereby hindering their leadership development. Fear is contagious, but courage or bravery is not. This may explain why hundreds of animals drinking water at a riverbank run helter-skelter at the sight of one single lion. All it takes is for one antelope to run upon sighting a lion, and the rest of the herd will follow and run in all directions. Most of the antelopes would not wait to see the lion before taking off. If all the antelopes would turn on the lion, and maybe even the lion's entire pride, the lion(s) would run away. However, the contagion effect of fear keeps the antelopes running away, consequently allowing the lion to chase and have a tasty lunch. To become a leader, the manager must learn to adopt the confidence and courage of the lion and should refrain from being an antelope. It takes courage to do the right thing in the face of various organizational constituents who want decisions to favor them.

Expanding the Zone of Indifference

The concepts of the zone of indifference and the zone of acceptance were already explained under the discussion of management characteristics. The concepts will not be re-explained here, but they are being revisited because of their importance and centrality to leadership. Because the actions of management focus on doing things right, as they are to be done (Bennis & Nanus, 2007), management actions maintain the subordinates' zones of indifference (Katz & Kahn, 1978). Also, remember that leadership is a process or an art of influencing others to achieve maximum performance (Lussier & Achua, 2023; Pride et al., 2008). Because leadership actions are about doing the right thing (Bennis & Nanus, 2007), leadership gets followers to expand their zones of indifference (Katz & Kahn, 1978). When employees are willing to do anything for you, when they come early and leave late to make sure that they perform their best each day, when they are willingly eager to do more than you ask of them, when they are happy to take your directives and even use their personal resources in the course of implementing your directives, in short, when they are willing to go to the moon and back to deliver on your request, they have expanded their zones of indifference for you (Barnard,

1938). This is the point expressed by Katz and Kahn (1978) when they said leadership was the influential increment in performance over and beyond the mechanical compliance with the instructions and expected performance dictated by organizational structure.

The point by Katz and Khan is that *leadership produces the increment in performance* beyond normal job expectations, which is a major distinguishing factor of leadership over management. In maintaining the zone of indifference, subordinates perform to the level of expectations consistently with an organizational mandate that they comply with the authority of the manager to perform at a satisfactory level. Subordinates take their cues from organizational expectations to give satisfactory or adequate performance, which may not necessarily be the best they can produce. To get additional productivity from subordinates beyond just the satisfactory level without any threat of punishment or promise of reward is the domain of leadership.

When the threat of punishment or an inducement of reward is used to get an employee to increase performance, such an approach for obtaining higher performance is management behavior rather than leadership. Also, whatever increased performance is obtained through managerial sanctions will last only as long as the sanctions remain in place. As soon as the sanction is lifted, either through managerial de-escalation of sanctions or forced removal of sanctions, which may be consequent to employee revolt, performance will revert to satisfactory levels at best or below satisfactory levels at worst. A below-satisfactory performance level may also occur as a retaliatory sabotage to management's sanction-centered style. However, managers who have become leaders will regularly get higher performance beyond satisfactory job expectations from their followers through influence.

Leadership influence, as discussed earlier, is not based on the use of sanctions but rather on the ability to consistently encourage followers to willingly expand their levels of the zone of indifference (Barnard,1938) or zone of acceptance if we are to use the positive language, acceptance, preferred by Herbert Simon (1997). This encouragement leads to increased productivity and self-actualization. The willing expansion of the zone of indifference or zone of acceptance is the ultimate outcome of leadership in organizations, as it generates higher performance from workers. In addition to increased productivity, the expansion of the zone of acceptance has the additional benefits of generating higher organizational engagement, better organizational citizenship, and commitment to the manager or organization.

The case of my soccer player, Josh, whom I mentioned earlier in this chapter, is a good example of the expansion of the zone of indifference or acceptance through leadership influence. Josh did not have to attend our soccer game that Saturday. He knew I would appoint another player to his position, and we would still probably win the game. Even if we did not win the game, our team was still at the top of the league, and losing one game would not have stopped us from winning the league. Even if we did not become league champions that year, we had been champions the previous two consecutive years and at other times in the past, so another championship victory would not have been novel to the team. Also, the city league was only recreational, so it carried no major consequences for losing or winning a game beyond bragging rights. Josh could have easily stayed in Denver and enjoyed the reception party at the wedding he was attending. He did not need to buy an airplane ticket and fly home for the game, but he did so just not to disappoint me. He expanded his zone of indifference or acceptance just for me. Leadership is about getting others, the followers, to willingly and joyfully expand their zones of indifference. People who refuse to willingly and happily expand their zones of indifference or acceptance have not accepted the manager as their leader. They remain subordinates rather than followers.

Voluntary Extraordinary Performance

Unlike management, which uses bureaucratic authority to get obedient compliance from subordinates, leadership gets voluntary willingness from followers for extraordinary performance. This refers to performance outcomes beyond ordinarily meeting job expectations and complying with job instructions, as earlier indicated by Katz and Kahn (1978). Leaders rely only on the use of influence granted to them by their followers, and they use their influence to create conditions in which followers become motivated to achieve extraordinary performance (Azizah, 2016). Followers are not bound by bureaucratic authority to take instructions from a leader. They do so because of their affection, admiration, respect, and reverence for the leader. This is a manager who the workers have made their leader. They have bestowed endorsed power on him to influence them. The success of leadership influence to get extraordinary performance weighs on the leader's ability to foster pride, faith, and respect in the followers (Sladjana, 2017). In addition, the leader taps into the reverence of endorsed power to excite idealized qualities and actions in the followers (Budur & Demir, 2019), resulting in exceptional performance outcomes. They eagerly take the leader's instructions and voluntarily align their interests with those of the leader for sentimental reasons rather than because of organizational sanctions. They are willing to cooperate with the leader out of respect and reverence for the person of the leader rather than for the position and privileges of managerial authority that the leader may simultaneously hold as a manager. This last point requires further explanation to prevent any confusion.

It is important to differentiate between voluntary willingness for extraordinary performance and voluntary compliance. Many management and leadership books erroneously characterize leadership as the attainment of voluntary compliance. This mischaracterization is a significant flaw in the explanation of leadership in these books. A closer look at these books would reveal how getting "voluntary compliance" is often included in the definitions and characteristics of leadership. This is the case in seminal leadership books like the one by Etzioni (1965) mentioned in Chapter Two of this book. Like other literature on leadership, Etzioni posited that leadership involves the ability of the leader to secure voluntary compliance (Etzioni, 1965). Contemporary books (such as Lussier & Achua, 2004) and more recent research articles (such as Pizzolitto et al., 2023; Huang et al., 2023) also typically make the same erroneous claim. I mentioned in Chapter Two that the issue of voluntary compliance would be addressed later in this book, and this is the appropriate place for that discussion.

The problem with associating leadership with voluntary compliance instead of non-coercive voluntary willingness for cooperation is that compliance cannot be voluntary. Compliance is a response to authority, rules, and regulations. One complies with rules, policies, and regulations under the directives of authority, which can reward compliance and inflict legitimate punishment for noncompliance. When a manager issues a directive, the directive is based on organizationally prescribed roles of both manager and subordinate for tasks that must be completed. Therefore, the directives are guided and supported by organizational authority and rules. The only expected and acceptable response to managerial directives or instructions, when issued consistently with organizational rules and backed by position authority, is compliance. So, if compliance is the only acceptable response, it cannot be voluntary. Even if the worker is granted room for dissent, the ultimate outcome of dissent is compliance or dismissal from the organization.

Getting compliance should always be recognized as an obedient phenomenon. It is not a voluntary act, and it is an error to associate it with leadership. The influencing nature of leadership does not carry organizational authority to coerce others to obey rules, and there is no organizational or bureaucratic backing for leadership influence. Leadership influence is fully an informal phenomenon based on affective feelings towards the person who is anointed as a leader by followers. It is important to keep in mind that *leadership is purely a relational influence* born out of human relations that generate social acceptance of someone as a leader apart from the person's managerial position (Wolinski, 2023). It also means that to remain a leader, one must maintain the pattern of relationship that produces leadership and followership (Wolinski, 2023).

Human Relations Techniques

Leadership is people-centric. While management uses management techniques, leadership uses human relations techniques. That is, the method of leadership is that of human relations. Unlike a common perception that having good human relations means one is nice and friendly, the use of human relations as a leadership competency implies much more than being nice or friendly. The human relations technique is an interactional approach whereby the worker is recognized as a whole human being and treated as such in the workplace. A human being is not a machine that does not have emotions or feel pain. Unlike machines, human beings feel pain. They get tired, they need rest, they get upset, they feel joy, they get sick, they need time for family, food, recreation, and social events, they value being appreciated, they have personal goals, they seek fairness, and many more things. The worker comes to the workplace each day with skills and experience, but also with feelings, problems, concerns, sadness, joy, hopes, emotions, and many other human conditions. Sometimes, workers come to work feeling depressed, and at other times, feeling on top of the world. One day, they perform flawlessly, and another day, they perform very poorly. In short, human beings come to the workplace with a myriad of complex needs and issues tugging at them from multiple directions.

By using human relations techniques, the leader takes the employee as a total package of the good, the bad, and the ugly. The leader collaborates well with the employee in the many dimensions of being human. This means the human relations technique puts the complexities of being human in the workplace into consideration in the coordination of work activities for goal attainment. Rather than using the authoritative command granted by organizational bureaucracy to get workers to perform, as a manager would do, a leader would relate with workers in ways that put their plight and conditions into consideration.

In the face of personal difficulties, a leader will influence workers to perform at their peak and not succumb to a suffocating situation. Through positive human relations techniques, the leader puts the conditions and attributes of workers into consideration when making decisions. This is especially necessary when decisions made directly affect workers' performance or well-being. This consideration demonstrates sensitivity to each employee's personal plight in any decision made, as well as signals that each employee is valued.

The key to the success of the human relations approach lies in the use of logic and science to know how to best relate with employees under different circumstances based on theories and principles of human behavior in society in general and organizations in particular. This is because the human relations technique is based on the sciences of human behavior rather than just being nice.

Vision Orientation

Vision orientation is a pivotal leadership competency; therefore, it is vital for managers to be vision-oriented to become leaders. A leader uses influence to guide a workgroup towards collective goals, envision what is possible, and strategize to achieve them. A leader must possess a clear vision of what can be accomplished beyond the current group performance, and, then, inspire group members to share this vision and work towards it. In essence, leadership involves effectively communicating and selling a vision to followers!

A vision is derived from asking the "what" and "why not" questions (Bennis, 1989). That is, after completing assigned and expected goals, a leader would ask what else is possible and why not achieve it. Why not achieve goal Z, an envisioned goal, if it is a meaningful achievement that will increase job satisfaction and contribute to meeting the needs of the organization and one's followers? A vision is about future possibilities that can excite others for additional accomplishments. A vision is a likely fulfillment of a potentially reachable goal in the future. It is about something that is currently absent but imagined as having contributive value if attained. This is an indication that the leader is someone who challenges the status quo, such as changing the suffocating condition, according to Warren Bennis (1989). While management focuses on achieving and maintaining the status quo (current conditions, even a suffocating one), leadership challenges it. Leadership attempts to exceed the status quo with a vision of innovative long-term plans and the development of structures and systems for additional goal accomplishments.

Being vision-oriented requires the leader to be able to sell a vision of higher possibilities to followers. This means that followers must be inspired or motivated to be part of the vision of the leader (Bennis, 1989), and the leader should use only intrinsic motivators (Bennis, 1989) to encourage voluntary participation in the accomplishment of the vision. Imagine this scenario. A captain and commandant of a military outfit took his men to a battle. After several hours of fighting, his men were able to fully decimate their opposition. They won the battle. But, instead of heading back to their camp, the commander noticed a hill on the horizon, and he discerned that if the hill fell into the hands of their enemies, it would prove disastrous for his side in the future. So, he rallied his soldiers together, explained the importance of the hill, and convinced them to capture the hill right away before it fell into the hands of the enemies. Because the control of the hill would save the lives of his men and other allied troops in the future, his men marshaled all their energy into going up the hill and occupying it. They were already exhausted and sustained injuries from the earlier battle, yet, they used every ounce of energy they had left to take the hill.

What the commander did by taking the hill was a demonstration of visioning as a leadership competence. Upon completing his assignment of winning a battle, he recognized the need to secure long-term safety for his soldiers by securing and controlling the hill. His official assignment was already completed with the battle. Taking the hill was not a part of his assigned duty, but his visioning led him to also take it. His troop followed him to take the hill, despite its tired condition, because it saw meaning and value in his vision. The soldiers aligned their personal interests in safety with the commander's need to provide collective safety. The commander's leadership behavior of visioning began with the question, "Why not?" Why not take the hill? Then, he provided logical and compelling reasons that created the motivation for his soldiers to buy into his vision. Each soldier's motivation was the intrinsic need for personal safety and being alive. This is consistent with Warren Bennis' claim that leadership requires the ability to inspire followers to willingly want to be part of the leader's vision based on intrinsic motivation (Bennis, 1989).

As demonstrated in my hypothetical scenario above, an important way to create intrinsic motivation, such as interest in a collective vision, is by aligning an organization's or group's visionary goals with the personal goals of the workers as much as possible. It is important to converge collective and individual interests. The Expectancy or Valence Theory of Victor Vroom (1964) supports this assertion. Vroom explained that an individual's intrinsic job motivation is derived from the person's perception of three conditions: 1) the degree to which increased efforts will produce desired outcomes (expectancy), 2) the degree to which rewards for attaining desired outcomes is strictly dependent on achieved outcomes (instrumentality), and 3) the value attached to the rewards obtained for achieved outcomes (valence). Hence, the likelihood of job motivation increases when: 1) workers believe additional efforts will produce higher job performance, 2) the reward for higher performance can only be obtained because of the higher performance, and 3) workers attach high value to the rewards given to them for attaining higher performance (House & Mitchell, 1975). While rewards for higher performance can be both extrinsic and intrinsic, it is the intrinsic type that produces intrinsic motivation, as Douglas McGregor (1906 [2006]) explained. By aligning a leader's vision of organizational or group goals with team members' goals, the wisdom of expectancy theory indicates that workers will buy into the vision and willingly participate to see it accomplished.

For individual group members to align their interests with the vision of a leader requires the leader to know group members well enough to know their personal motivation goals. Since motivation is internal to the individual, it will not be easily known without an active effort from the leader to pull it out of the workers. One way to do so is to actively listen to workers and discern their motives from the themes in their stories. It is the theme in their stories that will reveal their internal needs and goals since people are usually not able to readily explain or articulate their needs and goals (McClelland, 1971). Through the series of interactions that produce a leader-follower relationship, the leader would learn the theme in followers' needs and, hence, provide the path through which the needs can be achieved while at the same time achieving organizational goals.

The idea of leadership behavior that creates the path to goal achievement is the central focus of Robert J. House's Path-Goal Theory. Using the assumptions and propositions of this theory, subordinates are highly likely to buy into a leader-aspiring manager's vision when he engages in certain leadership behaviors such as (1) setting meaningful, desirable, and achievable goals within the control of workers, (2) connecting the personal satisfaction of workers to the unit's goal attainment, (3) helping workers clarify expectancies, (4) creating the right structure for the accomplishment of visioned goals, (5) convincing workers that the structure and goals are the paths to their job satisfaction, (6) eliminating or reducing barriers to goal achievement (7) coaching as necessary to make goal achievement as easy as possible, and (8) providing valued rewards for goal attainment (House, 1971).

An important takeaway about selling a vision is that it is beyond "telling" and expecting support, or worse, an obedient action. To tell and expect obedient compliance is management behavior rather than leadership. It is leadership behavior to make a logical, ethical, and emotionally appealing case for the importance of a vision. A vision should be based on likely intrinsic future benefits for a collective and the individual, and it should include the conditions that will make the attainment of the vision possible. This is when followers are likely to support a vision and act to achieve it, especially in their own best interest.

Provision of Protection

In the movie, *A Few Good Men*, Lieutenant Commander Joanne Galloway (actress Demi Moore) was asked a question in one of the courtroom scenes by her co-defending attorney, Lieutenant Junior Grade Sam Weinberg (Kevin Pollak), regarding the two soldiers that were on trial for the death of another soldier. The Lieutenant Commander was very enthusiastic about giving the accused soldiers a great defense, which led to a question that was posed to her by the Lieutenant Junior Grade. The question was: "Why do you like them so much?" And, the Lieutenant Commander replied with the sentence, "Because they stand on the wall. And they say, 'Nothing is gonna hurt you tonight.' Not on my watch". This is what leaders do! They stand on the wall. They stand guard. They watch over their followers. They say nothing will hurt you on their watch!

Leaders protect their followers. When higher organizational authorities make decisions that may negatively affect others, leaders step up to protect their command group members. Leaders will arrange meetings with higher management to discuss how their group members may be adversely affected by organizational actions and negotiate ways to shield them from the adverse effects. In some cases, to prevent harm to their followers, leaders will blatantly challenge organizational policies and actions at great risk to their own employment or personal benefits. I was made aware of the case of a very good district manager who was terminated in a big national retail store. For this example, I shall nickname this district manager, Gold. He had worked for the corporation for over 15 years with consistent distinction in his annual evaluations. In fact, he was hired because of his stellar management record from another national retail store. He reported to a regional manager that I shall call Silver. Both Gold and Silver got along very well. They were very friendly and cordial in their professional relationship. There was cordial mutual admiration and respect between the two men.

One day, both men got similar letters from the corporate office inviting them to separate meetings. Gold called his regional manager, Silver, to inquire about why he got the letter, but Silver did not have any answers for Gold because he (Silver) was also bewildered by his own letter. Both men had their meetings with the head of the corporation's human resources (HR), during which Gold was laid off due to corporate restructuring. He called Silver to tell him about his layoff and to say goodbye to a wonderful regional manager. This was when Silver said his own position had also been eliminated, but he was offered Gold's district position, which he had accepted. He said he felt sad for Gold and regretted the organization's decision. However, he was happy to still have a job with the organization, albeit a lesser one than he previously had.

What happened in the above true-life story was unfortunate for both men. One lost his job, and the other was retained in his subordinate's lower position. A lost leadership opportunity, however, was also embedded in the story. Silver knew that he was being offered the position of his own subordinate, and he took it. He acted simply as a manager vis-à-vis Gold. He passed off an opportunity to exhibit an important leadership quality. If a leader must protect his followers, Silver could have acted as a leader by protecting Gold from being laid off. The proper leadership behavior for Silver should have been a refusal to take Gold's job and to strongly advocate for Gold to be retained in his job, especially since it was the position of the regional manager that was eliminated. Leadership behavior in that scenario should have been for

Silver to tell the HR executive that if Gold's performance had been stellar, as his performance reviews had indicated for several consecutive years, then he (Gold) should be retained. And, it would be acceptable to him (Silver) to be laid off since his position was the one being eliminated. This is one way to stand guard: by standing on the proverbial wall and saying nothing will hurt you tonight. Nothing will hurt Gold under my watch! This idea is similar to the idea that the leader eats last.

In his book, *Leaders Eat Last: Why Some Teams Pull Together and Others Don't*, Simon Sinek (2017) describes how teams become strong, build solidarity, and perform well through the leadership behavior of allowing team members to come first. The book explained how higher group performance could result from a leadership expressive goal behavior that looked out for the well-being of the group, making sure that the conveniences of the group came first, and the interest of the leader came last. By eating last, leaders willingly put the interest, safety, opportunity, and success of their group members above their own. And, they do so without any motive for rewards or special recognition. When they eat last, leaders stand on the wall and protect their followers purely for altruism.

Managers do not have to strive to protect their subordinates from administrative harm. They are required to only do things right. They focus on making sure things are done well and on time to meet their goals. Managers rely on using their authority to punish and reward. In most cases, managers are the ones who fire employees or recommend that the Human Resource Director dismiss employees. Rather than protecting, supporting, guiding, counseling, or coaching as may be necessary to assist an employee in performing better, it is the manager who hurts the employee with bad evaluations, negative sanctions, or even dismissal. Rather than standing on the wall to protect the command group, the manager hurts members of the command group. This is not intended to chastise managers. It is merely an acknowledgment of the inherent nature and expectation of management to call out nonperforming or poorly performing workers for negative sanctions. Managers are not expected to stand on the wall. They are not expected to protect and defend a subordinate from harm by higher executives. Rather, managers are trained to expose and report underperforming subordinates. Managers who protect subordinates from harm have acquired a leadership behavior. When managers begin to stand guard at the wall and begin to say, nothing bad will happen to you under my watch, they are engaging in one leadership behavior. This behavior will also facilitate the transformation of subordinates into followers. This is another example of how management and leadership differ!

Good Political Skills

Leadership requires having good political skills to resolve difficult situations and to meet the diverse and likely opposing interests of followers. A manager who aspires to become a leader will benefit enormously by developing these skills. Unlike a manager, who can rely on bureaucratic authority to resolve problems, a leader relies purely on the use of influence, which does not carry the license of coercion of bureaucratic authority to get results. And, given that followership is purely voluntary, a leader must practice great diplomacy without lying or resorting to manipulation to meet the personal diverse and opposing interests of followers. A manager who is caught lying will easily lose respect and be denied endorsed power needed for influence. The same is true for a known manipulator. Political skills are about how to negotiate compromises, create common ground among workers of opposing interests, and unite them for cooperation rather than competition. And, if they should compete, the competition should be functional by focusing on how to best perform a duty in the best interests of the entire unit. An unhealthy (dysfunctional) competition will eventually cause some members of the command group who have become followers to revert to subordinate status and simultaneously revert the leader to manager.

It can be expected that sooner or later, followers will differ in their decisions and outcome preferences. In some cases, the preferences of some followers may be perceived by another set of followers as infringing upon their own preferred outcomes, causing the followers to be divided into two camps of vested interest and veto groups. The leader's current decisions favor the vested interest group, and it would advocate for such decisions to continue. The group is vested in the current state of things. However, the veto group prefers a change in decisions and would like the leader to make only the decisions that it prefers (Veblen, 2022). By opposing the vested interest group, the veto group is advocating for its own interests in the leader's decision. While different perspectives are inevitable among followers, a strong division of interests is counterproductive to leadership success.

A division among followers is never in the best interest of a leader because leadership is sustained by the ability to continue to get endorsed power, which a split among the followers will jeopardize. To support or be perceived as supporting one side of the divide can easily erode the belief in the leader's ability to make good judgments without bias. Trust in the leader may be questioned by one or even both factions of competing followers. This is a condition that I call the *landmine dilemma of leadership*, and it requires the leader to know how to best side-step this landmine through the effective application of political and human relations skills. To be a leader is to become adept at the politics of side-stepping the human relations landmine of competing factions and keeping one's team united in strong solidarity, working well together, and moving in the same direction. This requires vigilance on the part of the leader to use human relations to discover when followers have different perspectives about work processes and skillfully align their interests with those of the unit and organizational mission.

CHAPTER 6

OVERVIEW AND TAKEAWAYS

Bringing Everything Together

Core Ideas and Takeaways

REVISITING HEADSHIP

The Management Factor

There is no group without a head. Whether it is a corporation or corporate unit, a friendship group, a family, a delinquent gang, a committee, a church, or any other group, someone will occupy the status of the head of the group. So, inherent in a group or an organization existence is a head! However, headship is a generic term that must be understood in its different forms. This book guides the understanding of three major forms of headship and how to differentiate them. The head could be a ruler, a manager, or a leader. As discussed in Chapter One, the conflation of these concepts is a common phenomenon, and it is important to avoid it. It is necessary to avoid conflating headship with leadership since neither the ruler nor the manager is a leader. As a misnomer, the group head is often referred to as the group leader. This is a common reference error. This error is so pervasive that even when leadership authors distinguish between management and leadership, they often slip into referring to management as leadership. This error has become a standard that I term *commonly accepted standard error* (CASE) of leadership. As this book explains, just because one is the head of a group does not mean that one is leading the group.

This book is also intended to serve as a quick and user-friendly guide for understanding the functions and principles of management, which managers often overlook. In addition, the fundamental characteristics of management are well discussed to allow a group head to recognize the behaviors that make him or her a manager instead of a ruler or leader. The management characteristics that were discussed provide a solid foundation for anyone interested in the basics of management, especially with a special focus on the landmark works of Henri Fayol on management. Understanding the concepts and ideas discussed on management is a key step toward becoming an effective manager.

The main point of the discussion on management is to have a clear understanding of what management is, and to be able to differentiate it from leadership. As demonstrated in the characteristics of management, it is an essential part of any organization if an organization is to survive and thrive. The concept of organization inherently implies the presence of multiple people engaged in a common endeavor achieved through organizing. Organizational members must be organized in a systematic fashion that will allow the accomplishment of an organization's goals. If organizational members are to be organized for a common purpose, they cannot be at the same level or do the same thing. At least in the interest of efficiency, they will need to perform different activities that will yield their common goals. Among the various activities they will perform is management. Through management, all the activities that will result in the accomplishment of organizational goals are designed, distributed to others to perform, and coordinated. Managerial actions make organizational goals possible to accomplish; hence, management is necessary for organizational success. It is not an aspect of organizational design that is subject to dismissal. It is, therefore, important to recognize the characteristics of management if one is to be an effective manager. An effective manager obtains the expected standard performance and goal accomplishment from subordinates to meet a unit's contributions to overall organizational success.

The Leadership Factor

While management is crucial for achieving organizational success, it is still not leadership. But, to understand leadership, a strong understanding of management is important. Management gives us a benchmark or a starting point for understanding and assessing how to coordinate the activities of organizational members toward organizational objectives and goals. When the manager becomes a leader, he is able to achieve these goals through influence rather than managerial techniques and authority.

The preceding chapter discusses the meaning and the essential behavioral competencies of leadership. That chapter is the main reason for writing this book as it explains and discusses the qualities that make someone a leader for comparison and contrast with management, which was discussed in Chapters Three and Four.

While many definitions may exist for leadership, the most distinguishing feature of leadership is the use of non-coercive influence to guide others to accomplish managerial goals. Responsibilities for achieving organizational goals can only be assigned to managers because they occupy the positions that are officially designated for such purposes. After becoming a leader, the manager is able to use leadership influence to achieve the goals of his official managerial status. While all forms of group headships coordinate the efforts of others toward goal attainment, leadership is the only one that does it without the use of position authority. In place of bureaucratic authority, a leader coordinates the efforts of others, the followers, through influence, which is gained through interpersonal relations. Therefore, becoming a leader requires engaging with others in interactions that will result in gaining influence rather than relying on authority to accomplish goals.

It is especially well articulated and emphasized that leadership does not involve a response to someone based on the person's ability to reward or punish others. Also, leadership does not refer to an official position within an organizational structure. Rather, leadership is the outcome of good human relations that grants the leader the power of influence in coordinating the labor of the followers to accomplish organizational goals beyond adherence to expected performance levels. To be a leader is to be able to influence, inspire, or motivate others to achieve extraordinary outcomes. These are outcomes beyond an expected or acceptable level of performance. It is to be able to influence others to eagerly aspire to do more just for the leader. Leadership makes workers to self-actualize. As Maria Vasilescu put it, leaders provide an environment where followers are able to realize the very best of their abilities and initiatives (Vasilescu, 2019). The influence of a leader makes followers to eagerly work and consistently deliver top-level performance. While a good manager may use management techniques to get subordinates to meet goal expectations, the leader's influence, based on technical human relations skills, gets followers to achieve beyond merely meeting standard goal expectations. This is because leadership inspires and motivates followers to willingly and voluntarily expand their zones of indifference or acceptance.

Leadership is what makes others want to do more beyond expectations without any threat of punishment or promise of reward. When others do more just to please or impress you without any force or inducement for performance, you have become a leader to such persons. But the relativity of leadership is important. While one may be a leader to some workers, one may not be a leader to others in the same unit. This is because only those who have become followers among the subordinates in a workgroup transform the manager into a leader, their leader. To the subordinates who have not become followers, the group head remains a manager to them. Therefore, a manager becomes a leader only at the pleasure of the followers.

Those who become followers grant the manager the endorsed power to influence them beyond their zones of indifference. When this happens, they have made the manager their leader. It is the workers who control endorsed power. They can give it, and they can take it back. When they give it, the manager becomes their leader, and when they withdraw it, she reverts to being a manager, and the followers also revert to subordinates. Reverting to subordinate status means that the followers no longer wish to continue to expand their zones of indifference or acceptance, and therefore, they will only work to meet job expectations in exchange for their compensation. This typically happens because the leader's behaviors have fallen short of leadership qualities. The leader, perhaps, has reverted to exhibiting mostly managerial behaviors, which has also caused followers to revert to subordinate actions. This means that leaders must continuously use human relations skills to retain endorsed power in order to uninterruptedly retain and influence their followers. It also shows that leadership is an informally granted status under the control of followers rather than a bureaucratic organizational position like management, which the organization controls.

An important lesson about the informal status of leadership is that leadership education must include a separation of management positions from leadership. As explained in Chapter One, it is too common for leadership training to refer to managers and top corporate executives as leaders. By doing so, leadership is undermined and reduced to management. While management may be effective in accomplishing organizational goals, there are reasons why managers and executives attend leadership workshops. They attend leadership workshops mostly to learn leadership behaviors they need to practice in order to attain leadership competency. They obtain leadership education mainly because their organizations recognize the superiority of leadership over management in expanding workers' zones of indifference. Being leaders will result in greater employee performance than just meeting job expectations. Until management and leadership are correctly fully understood and distinguished from each other, and the differences between the two are fully internalized, the transformation of managers into leaders will always be hindered. To this end, I encourage leadership instructors, including those who conduct leadership workshops, to fully differentiate between managerial and leadership behaviors and emphasize the acquisition of leadership competency to enhance self-actualization among workers.

CITED WORKS

Adams, J. S. (1963).
Toward an Understanding of Equity. *Journal of Abnormal and Social Psychology*, November, 422–36.

Adams, J. S. (1965).
Inequity in Social Exchange. New York NY: Academic Press.

African Elections Data Base. (1979, July).
State Assembly Elections in Nigeria.
https://africanelections.tripod.com/ng_1979assembly.h tml#Ondo_State -July 21, (Accessed December 12, 2022)

Angell, M. (1999, July/August).
What Is a Good Decision? *Effective Clinical Practice, 2*(4), 186-187.

Anisa, C. A. (2020).
Konsep Kepemimpinan Otoriter Dalam Lembaga Pendidikan Di Sekolah atau Madrasah (The Concept of Authoritarian Leadership in Educational Institutions at Schools or Madrasahs). *Leadership: Journal Mahasiswa Manajemen Pendidikan Islam* (*Journal of Islamic Education Management Students*), 1(2), 155.

Aragon-Correa, J.A., Garcia-Morales, V.J., & Cordon-Pozo, E. (2007).
Leadership and organizational learning's role on innovation and performance: lessons from Spain, Industrial Marketing Management, 36(3), 349-59.

Armstrong, M. (2003).
A Handbook of Management Techniques, 3rd ed., London: UK: Kogan Page Limited.

Azizah, F. (2016).
The Influence of Leadership Style Principal Transformational and Work Motivation Teachers against Teacher Performance at SMA Al-Islam 1 Surakarta. Master's Thesis. Sebelas Maret University.

Bacharach, S. & Lawler, E. J. (1980).
Power and Politics in Organizations. San Francisco, CA: Jose Bass.

Barnard, C. I. (1938).
The Functions of the Executive. Cambridge, MA: Harvard University Press.

Bass, B. M. (1990).
Bass and Stogdill's Handbook of Leadership: Theory, Research and Managerial Applications (Vol. 3). New York: Free Press.

Bennis, W. G. (1989).
Managing the Dream: Leadership in the 21st Century. *Journal of Organizational Change Management*, 2(1), 6-10.

Bennis, W. G., & Nanus, B. (2007).
Leaders: The Strategies for Taking Charge. New York, NY: Harper Collins.

Bennis, W. G., & Nanus, B. (1985).
Leaders: The Strategies for Taking Charge. San Francisco: Harper Collins.

Brevis, T. (2014).
The Management Process. In T. Brevis & M. Vrba, (Eds.). *Contemporary Management Principles* (pp. 28-45). Claremont, South Africa: Juta and Company, Ltd.

Budur, T. & Demir, A. (2019).
Leadership Effects on Employee Perception bout CSR in Kurdistan Region of Iraq. *International Journal of Social Sciences and Educational Studies*, 6(1)142-154.

Burns, T. & Stalker, G.M. (1961).
The Management of Innovation. London, England: Tavistock Publications.

Chan, S.C.H., Huang, X., Snape, E., & Lam, C.K. (2013).
The Janus Face of Paternalistic Leaders: Authoritarianism, Benevolence, Subordinates' Organization-Based Self-Esteem, and Performance. *Journal of Organizational Behavior*, 34, 108–128.

Chiang, J.T.J., Chen, X.P., Liu, H., Akutsu, S., & Wang, Z. (2020).
We Have Emotions but Can't Show Them! Authoritarian Leadership, Emotion Suppression Climate, and Team Performance. *Human Relations* 74:1082–1111.

Conger, J. (1992).
Learning to Lead. San Francisco, CA: Jossey-Bass.

Crossman, A. (2020).
Expressive Roles and Task Roles. *ThoughtCo,* https://www.thoughtco.com/expressive-roles-definition-3026318 (Accessed, August 27, 2020).

Davis, R. C. (1951).
The Fundamentals of Top Management. New York: Harper and Brothers.

de Hoogh, A. H., Greer, L., & den Hartog, D. (2015).
Diabolical Dictators or Capable Commanders? An Investigation of the Differential Effects of Autocratic Leadership on Team Performance. *Leadership Quarterly,* 26,687–701.

Dornbusch, S. & Scott, W. R. (1975).
Evaluation and the Essence of Authority. New York, NY: Basic Books.

Dow, R. (1999, July/August). What Is a Good Decision? *Effective Clinical Practice, 2*(4), 187.
Etzioni, A. (1965). Dual Leadership in Complex Organization. *American Sociological Review, 30,* 688-698.

Farh, J.L. & Cheng, B.S. (2000).
A cultural Analysis of Paternalistic Leadership in Chinese Organizations. In J.T. Li, A.S. Tsui, & E. Weldon (Eds.). *Management and Organizations in the Chinese Context,* (pp. 94–127). London, UK: Palgrave Macmillan.

Farh, J.L., Cheng, B.S., Chou, L.F., Chu, X. (2006).
Authority and Benevolence: Employee's Responses to Paternalistic Leadership in China. In A.S. Tsui, Y. Bian, & L. Cheng. (Eds.). *China's Domestic Private Firms: Multidisciplinary Perspectives on Management and Performance,* (pp. 230–260). New York, NY: M.E. Sharpe.

Fayol, H. (2013 *original 1917*).
General and Industrial Management. (Translated by Constance Storrs from the French Edition). Mansfield Centre, CT: Martino Fine Publishing.

Fiedler, F. E. (1964).
Contingency Model of Leadership Effectiveness. *Advances in Experimental Social Psychology,* 1, 49–190.

Fiedler, F. E. (1972).
How Do You Make Leaders More Effective: New Answers to an Old Puzzle. *Organizational Dynamics,* 1, 3–8.

Guo, L., Decoster, S., Babalola, M.T., De Schutter, L., Garba, O.A., & Riisla, K. (2018).
Authoritarian Leadership and Employee Creativity: The Moderating Role of Psychological Capital and the Mediating Role of Fear and Defensive Silence. *Journal of Business Research,* 2018, 92, 219–230.

Fox, S., Spector, P. E., & Miles, D. (2001).
Counterproductive Work Behavior (CWB) in Response to Job Stressors and Organizational Justice: Some

Mediator and Moderator Tests for Autonomy and Emotions. *Journal of Vocational Behavior*, 59, 291–309.

Gardner, J. (2000).
The Nature of Leadership. *In The Josey-Bass Reader on Educational Leadership.* (pp. 3-120), ERIC Number: ED 443162. San Francisco: Jossey-Bass.

Gibson, J. L., Ivancevich, J. M. Donnelly, J. H., & Konopaske, R. (2012).
Organizations: Behavior, Structure and Processes, 14th ed. Boston: McGraw-Hill

Guinier, L. (1994).
The Tyranny of the Majority: Fundamental Fairness in Representative Democracy. New York, NY: The Free Press.

Halloran, J. & Benton D. (1987).
Applied Human Relations: An Organizational Approach. Englewood Cliffs, NJ: Prentice Hall, Inc.

Herzberg, F., Mausner, B. & Snyderman, B. (1959).
The Motivation to Work. New York, NY: John Wiley & Sons.

Hou, N., & Peng, J. (2019).
Authoritarian-Benevolent Leadership, Active Implementation, and Job Performance: An Investigation on the Effectiveness of Ambidextrous Leadership in the Chinese Context. *Acta Psychological Sinica.* 51(1), 117–127.

House, R. J. (1971).
A Path-Goal Theory of Leadership Effectiveness. *Administrative Science Quarterly,* 16, 321–339

House, R. J., & Mitchell, T. R. (1975).
Organizational Effectiveness Research Programs Office of Naval Research. *Technical Report* 75-67, April 1975. https://apps.dtic.mil/sti/pdfs/ADA009513.pdf (Accessed December 17, 2022).

Huang, Q., Zhang, K., Wang, Y., Bodla, A.A., & Zhu, D. (2023).
When Is Authoritarian Leadership Less Detrimental? The Role of Leader Capability. *International Journal of Environmental Research in Public Health* 20, 707.

Hughes, R., Ginnett, R., & Curphy, G. (1999).
Leadership: Enhancing the Lessons of Experience. Boston, MA: Irwin/McGraw-Hill.

Isonen, O. (2016, October 29).
Professional Deformation (Distortion). https://oleg008.medium.com/professional-deformation-distortion-7eb8d88b562a (Accessed March 8, 2021).

Ivancevich, J. M., Konopaske, R., & Matteson, M. (2014).
Organizational Behavior and Management. New York, NY: McGraw-Hill Irwin.

Ivancevich, J. M. & Duening, T. N. (2007).
Business: Principles, Guidelines, and Practices. Mason, OH: Atomic Dog Publishing.

Karakitapoglu-Aygün Z., Gumusluoglu, L., Erturk, A., & Scandura, T. A. (2021).
Two to Tango? A Cross-Cultural Investigation of the Leader-Follower Agreement on Authoritarian Leadership. *Journal of Business Research*, 128:473–485.

Katz, D. & Kahn, R. L. (1978).
The Sociology Psychology of Organizations. Revised Edition. New York, NY: Wiley.

Kelloway, E. K., Sivanathan, N., Francis, L., & Barling, J. (2005).
Poor Leadership. In J. Barling, E. K. Kelloway & M. R. Frone (Eds.). *Handbook of Work Stress (Chapter 5).* Thousand Oaks, CA: Sage.

Koontz, H. & O'Donnell, C. (1968).
Principles of Management: An Analysis of Managerial Functions, 4th Ed. New York, NY: McGraw-Hill

Koveshnikov, A., Ehrnrooth, M. & Wechtler, H. (2022).
Authoritarian and Benevolent Leadership: The Role of Follower Homophily, Power Distance Orientation and Employability, *Personnel Review*, 51(1), 218-235.

Krishali, S. (2021).
What Are the Functions of Management?
https://www.economicsdiscussion.net/management/7-functions-of-management/31965 [Accessed Feb 13, 2021].

Lee, A., Legood, A., Hughes, D., Tian, A. W., Newman, A., & Knight, C. (2019).
Leadership, Creativity, and Innovation: A Meta-Analytic Review. *European Journal of Work & Organizational Psychology*, 29,1–35.

Li, R., Chen, Z., Zhang, H., & Luo, J. (2019).
How Do Authoritarian Leadership and Abusive Supervision Jointly Thwart Follower Proactivity? A Social Control Perspective. *Journal of Management,* 47,930–956.

Li, G., Rubenstein, A. L., Lin, W., Wang, M., & Chen, X. (2018).
The Curvilinear Effect of Benevolent Leadership on Team Performance: The Mediating Role of Team Action Processes and the Moderating Role of Team Commitment. *Personnel Psychology*, 71, 369–397.

Leymann, H. (1996).
The Content and Development of Mobbing at Work. *European Journal of Work and Organizational Psychology*, 5, 165–184.

Lowe, K.B., Kroeck, K.G., & Sivasubramaniam, N. (1996).
Effectiveness Correlates of Transformational and Transactional Leadership: A Meta-Analytic Review of the MLQ Literature. *Leadership Quarterly*, 7(3), 385-425.

Lussier, R. A. & Achua, C. F. (2023).
Leadership: Theory, Application, and Skill Development, 7th ed. Thousand Oaks, CA: Sage Publications Inc.

Management Basics. (2024).
Management As a Group. https://www.managementstudyguide.com/management _group.htm (Accessed August 24, 2024).

Mayo, E. (1946).
The Human Problems of an Industrial Civilization. Cambridge, MA: Harvard Press.

McClelland, D. C. (1971).
Motivational Trends in Society. Morristown, NJ: General Learning Press.

McCormack, K. (2014).
Ethos, Pathos, and Logos: The Benefits of Aristotelian Rhetoric in the Courtroom. *Washington University Jurisprudence Review.* 7, 131-155.

McGregor, D. (2006 *original 1906*).
The Human Side of Enterprise. Annotated Edition. New York, NY: McGraw-Hill

Meindl, J. R., Ehrlich, S. B. & Dukerich, J. M. (1985).
The Romance of Leadership. *Administrative Science Quarterly,* 30, 78-102.

Meng, L., Li, T., Yang, M., & Wang, S. (2022).
A study on the Influence of Authoritarian-Benevolent Leadership on Employees' Innovative Behavior from the Perspective of Psychological Perception-Based on Fuzzy Set Qualitative Comparative Analysis. *Frontiers in Psychology.* doi:10.3389/ fpsyg.2022.886286

Merriam-Webster Dictionary.
(https://www.merriam-webster.com/dictionary/labor).
(Accessed July 7, 2022).

Merton, R. K. (1968).
Social Theory and Social Structure. New York, NY: The Free Press.

Merton, R. K. (1936).
The Unanticipated Consequences of Purposive Social Action. *American Sociological Review*, 1, 894-904.

Metz, H. C., ed. (1991).
Nigeria: A Country Study. Washington: GPO for the Library of Congress. http://countrystudies.us/nigeria/ (Accessed July 25, 2022).

Meyer, J. P. & Allen, N. J. (1991).
A Three-Component Theory of Organizational Structure. *Human Resource Management Review*, 1(1), 61-89.

Miller, G. A. (1967).
Professionals in Bureaucracy, Alienation Among Industrial Scientists and Engineers. *American Sociological Review*, 32, 755-768.

Mshvenieradze, T. (2013).
Logos, Ethos, and Pathos in Political Discourse. *Theory and Practice in Language Studies*, 3(11), 1939-1945.

Ofstad, H. (1961). *An Inquiry into the Freedom of Decision.* Sydney, Australia: Allen and Unwin.

Ondo State House of Assembly, 1979-1983. https://africanelections.tripod.com/ng_1979assembly.h tml#Ondo_State (Accessed July 25, 2022).

Oyinlade, A. O., & Christo, Z. J. (2020). Path Analysis Between Organizational Size and Forms of Organizational Commitment. *American Journal of Industrial and Business Management*, 10, 1655-1680.

Oyinlade, A. O., Gellhaus, M., & Darboe, K. (2003). Essential Leadership Qualities for Effective Leadership in Schools for Students Who are Visually Impaired: A National Study. *Journal of Visual Impairment & Blindness*, 97(7), 389-402.

Parsons, T. (1966). *Societies: Evolutionary and Comparative Perspectives.* Englewood Cliffs, NJ: Prentice Hall.

Pellegrini, E.K., & Scandura, T.A. (2008). Paternalistic Leadership: A Review and Agenda for Future Research. *Journal of Management*, 34, 566–593.

Perackovic, K. (2011). Division of Labor in Some Classical Concepts—An Attempt of Contemporary Theoretical Synthesis. *Journal des Economistes et des Etudes Humaines:* 17(1) Article 1.

Peters, T. & Austin, N. (1985). *A Passion for Excellence: The Leadership Difference.* New York, NY: Warner Books.

Pizzolitto, E., Verna, I., & Venditti, M. (2023). Authoritarian Leadership Styles and Performance: A Systematic Literature Review and Research Agenda. *Management Review Quarterly,* 73, 841–871.

Postema, G. J. (2001). Law as Command: The Model of Command in Modern Jurisprudence. *Philosophical Issues,* 11, 470-501.

Pride, W. M., Hughes, R. J., & Kapoor, J. R. (2008). *Business.* Boston, MA: Houghton Mifflin.

Purwanto, A., Asbari, M., Santoso, P. B., Wijayanti, L. M., Hyun, C. C., Sihite, O. B., & Saifuddin, M. P. (2020). The Effect of Participatory and Autocratic Leadership Style on the Performance of the HAS 23000 Halal Assurance System in the Packaged Food Industry. *Edumaspul: Journal of Education,* 4(1), 156–179.

Ratliff, A. (1999). What Is a Good Decision? *Effective Clinical Practice,* 2(4), 185-186.

Rahmani, M., Roles, G., & Karmarkar, U.S. (2018). Team Leadership and Performance: Combining the Roles of Direction and Contribution. *Management Science,* 64, 5234–5249.

Ridgeway, C. L. (1983). *The Dynamics of Small Groups.* New York, NY: St. Martin's Press.

Rodrigues, C. (2001). *International Management: A Cultural Approach.* Cincinnati, OH: South-Western College Publishing.

Sagie, A. (1996).
Effects of Leader's Communication Style and Participative Goal Setting on Performance and Attitudes. *Human Performance*, 9, 51–64.

Sanchez-Manzanares, M., Rico, R., Antino, M., & Uitdewilligen, S. (2020).
The Joint Effects of Leadership Style and Magnitude of the Disruption on Team Adaptation: A Longitudinal Experiment. *Group & Organization Management*, 45, 836–864.

Schaubroeck, J. M., Shen, Y., Chong, S. (2017).
A Dual-Stage Moderated Mediation Model Linking Authoritarian Leadership to Follower Outcomes. *Journal of Applied Psychology*, 102, 203–214.

Sevel, M. (2018).
Obeying the Law. *Legal Theory*, 24, 191–215.

Simon, H. A. (1997 *original 1947*).
Administrative Behavior: A Study of Decision-Making Processes in Administrative Organizations (4th ed.). New York: Free Press.

Sinek, S. (2017).
Leaders Eat Last: Why Some Teams Pull Together and Others Don't. Paperback Ed. New York, NY: Portfolio-Penguin Book.

Sladjana, S. (2017).
The Impact of Dimensions of TL on Post-Acquisition Performance of Acquired Company. *Economic Horizons*, 19(2) 95-108.

Smith, A. (1985 *original 1776*).
An Inquiry into the Nature and Causes of the Wealth of Nations. New York: Modern Library.

Steers, R. M., Porter, L., & Bigley, G. (1996).
Motivation and Leadership at Work, 6th ed. New York: McGraw-Hill.

Stein, L. (2016).
Schools Need Leaders - Not Managers: It's Time for a Paradigm Shift. *Journal of Leadership Education, 15* (2), 21-30.

Stogdill, R. M. (1974).
Handbook of Leadership. New York: The Free Press.

Tannenbaum, R., Weschler, I.R., & Massarik, F. (1961). *Leadership and Organization,* McGraw-Hill, New York, NY.

Taylor, F. (1997 *original 1911*).
Principles of Scientific Management. Mineola, NY: Dover Publications.

Terry, G. R. (1977).
Principles of Management. Burr Ridge, Ill: R.D. Irwin Publisher.

Tolbert, P., & Hall, R. (2016).
Organizations: Structures, Processes and Outcome, 10th ed. New York, NY: Routledge.

Uhl-Bien, M., Riggio, R.E., & Lowe, K.B. (2014).
Carsten, M.K. Followership Theory: A Review and Research Agenda. *Leadership Quarterly*, 25, 83–104.

Vasilescu, M. (2019).
Leadership Styles and Theories in an Effective Management Activity. *Annals of the Constantin Brancusi, Economic Series*, 4, 47-52.

Veblen, T. (2022, *original 1919*).
The Vested Interests and the Common Man. Teotihuacan, Mexico: Legare Street Press.

Veblen, T. (2019, *original 1914*).
The Instinct of Workmanship and the State of the Industrial Arts. Chicago, IL: E-Artnow publisher.

Vroom, V., H., (1964).
Work and Motivation. New York, NY: John Wiley & Sons.

Wang, A. C., Chiang, J. T. J., Tsai, C. Y., Lin, T. T., & Cheng, B. S. (2013).
Gender Makes the Difference: The Moderating Role of Leader Gender on the Relationship Between Leadership Styles and Subordinate Performance. *Organizational Behavior and Human Decision Process*, 122, 101–113.

Watson, J. B. (1930).
Behaviorism (Revised Edition). Chicago, IL: University of Chicago Press.

Weber, M. (1947 *original 1908*).
The Theory of Social and Economic Organization. New York: Free Press.

Weber, M. (2010 *original 1904-05*).
The Protestant Ethic and the Spirit of Capitalism. Revised and translated by Stephen Karlberg. New York: Oxford University Press, Inc.

White, R. & Lippitt, D. (1953).
Leader Behavior in Three Social Climates. In Dorwin Cartwright and Alvin Zander (Eds.), *Group Dynamics* (pp. 586-611). Evanston, Ill: Row and Peterson.

Wolinski, S. (2023).
Leadership Defined. All About Leadership Books: How Do I Lead? *Management Library.*
http://managementhe.org/blogs/leadership/2010/04/2 1/leadership-theories/ (Accessed May 20, 2024).

Wood, J. (2013).
Organizational Behavior: Core Concepts and Applications (3rd.). Milton, Qld.: John Wiley and Sons Australia.

World Bank Data. (2021).
GDP: All Countries and Economies. https://data.worldbank.org/indicator/NY.GDP.MKTP.C D?most_recent_value_desc=false(Accessed October 14, 2022).

Wu, M., Huang, X., & Chan, S.C.H. (2012a).
The Influencing Mechanisms of Paternalistic Leadership in Mainland China. *Asia and Pacific Business Review* 18, 631–648.

Wu, M., Huang, X., Li, C., & Liu, W. (2012b). Perceived Interactional Justice and Trust-In-Supervisor as Mediators for Paternalistic Leadership. *Management & Organization Rev*iew, 8, 97–121.

Yao, L., Chen, X., & Wei, H. (2022). How do Authoritarian and Benevolent Leadership Affect Employee Work-Family Conflict? An Emotional Regulation Perspective. *Asia and Pacific Journal of Management*, 4, 1–29.

Yukl, G., Lepsinger, R., & Lucia, A. (1992). Preliminary Report on the Development and Validation of the Influence Behavior Questionnaire. In K.E. Clark, M.B. Clark & D. Campbell (Eds.), *The Impact Leadership* (pp. 417-427). Greensboro, NC: Center for Creative Leadership.

Yun, S., Faraj, S., & Sims, H. P. (2005). Contingent Leadership and Effectiveness of Trauma Resuscitation Teams. *Journal of Applied Psychology,* 90, 1288–1296.

Yun, S., Cox, J., Henry, P., & Sims Jr., H.P. (2006) The Forgotten Follower: A Contingency Model of Leadership and Follower Self-Leadership. *Journal of Managerial Psychology*, 21, 374-388.

Zhang, Y. & Xie, Y. (2017). Authoritarian Leadership and Extra-Role Behaviors: A Role-Perception Perspective. *Management and Organization Review*, 13, 147–166.

INDEX

A

A Few Good Men 207
About the Author 251
Absolute Authority 49
Achua ..... xiv, 54, 59, 190, 196, 233
Acknowledgements.............xii
Adam Smith .... See Smith
Adams.........................97, 225
African Elections Data Base 38, 225
Allen 154, 235
An Inquiry into the Nature and Causes of the Wealth of Nations................76, 239
Angell..................177, 178, 225
Anisa.......................... 124, 225
Anna Jensen........................xi
Aragon-Correa 28, 226
Are you a ruler, a manager, or a leader? 35
Are you a ruler, manager, or leader?..........................xvii
Aristotle............................ 160
Armstrong 120, 121, 226
Austin 27, 44, 45, 236
Authoritarian ruler ...... xix, 54
Authoritarianism ...49, 53, 54, 122, 123, 124, 227
Authoritative command 54, 124, 199

Authoritative Management Technique 122
Authorized Power 114
Azizah 194, 226

B

Bacharach...................115, 226
Barnard 108, 136, 138, 157, 190, 192, 226
Bass 131, 226, 228, 230
Bennis...57, 134, 135, 172, 173, 180, 190, 201, 202, 203, 226, 227
Benton . 44, 125, 128, 129, 131, 174, 230
Bisi... xi
Branden Mitchel xi
Brevis........................108, 227
Bryan Holzhey xi
Budur........................ 195, 227
Bureaucracy . 72, 133, 147, 183
Bureaucratic Activities and Status............................. 132
Bureaucratic Authority......114
Bureaucratic Managerial Authority....................... 169
Burns 94, 227

C

Carrie Lacy xi
CASESee Commonly accepted standard error, See

Commonly accepted standard error, See Commonly accepted standard error
Centralization 89
Chan 51, 227, 241
Cheng ... 48, 52, 228, 229, 240
Chiang 49, 51, 227, 240
Christo ....xi, 154, 236
Christopher Achua xiv
Cited Works 225
Command Group ... 83, 84, 92, 94, 113, 114, 125, 127, 128, 130, 163, 164, 207, 211, 213
Commanding 68
Commonly accepted standard error 25, 147, 217
Compliance . 117, 118, 169, 196
Conflation 23, 24, 25, 43, 147, 216
Conger 57, 58, 228
Consultative Approach-Decision-Making 125
Content Layout 30
Contents vii
Contingency Theory 52, 55
Controlling 73
Controlling Function of Management 73
Core Ideas and Takeaways 215
Courage . 184, See Leadership: Courage
Crossman 111, 228

D

Daniel Warnotte 181
David Finch xi
Davis 74, 228
de Hoogh 51, 55, 228
Deanne Barrett xi

Decision ... 49, 50, 54, 93, 120, 125, 127, 128, 132, 174, 176, 177, 178, 179, 182, 186, 187, 188, 200, 213
Dedication xi
Demir 195, 227
Democratic Approach-Decision-Making ... 125, 126
Differentiating Among Concepts 35
Directing 69
Division of Labor 75, 76, 77, 78, 183
Doing Things Right 134
Dornbusch .. 114, 117, 157, 228
Dow 177, 178, 179, 228
Duening 69, 231
Dysfunctions of Rulership .. 51

E

Emma Eitzmann xv
Endorsed Power . 156, 157, 158
Equity 96, 225
Esprit de corps 102, 103
Essentials of Management Functions and Principles 62
Ethos ... See Leadership: Ethos
Etzioni .. 58, 158, 170, 196, 228
Expectancy or Valence Theory 204
Expressive goals 110
External Organizational Environment 186

F

Farh 48, 49, 52, 228, 229
Fayol ... 26, 62, 63, 64, 65, 68, 70, 73, 74, 75, 76, 79, 80, 82, 83, 84, 86, 87, 88, 89,

91, 92, 94, 95, 96, 99, 101, 102, 103, 115, 120, 217, 229
Fear............................189, 229
Fiedler 55, 229
Financial Management......121
Followers Determine Their Leaders!...........................141
Followership .See Leadership: Followership
Fox............................. 131, 229
Frederick Taylor ....See Taylor
Frederick Winslow Taylor See Taylor
Functions of Management . 63

G

Gardner 55, 57, 230
General Management 121
George R. Terry....... See Terry
Gerry Cox xiv
Gibson 54, 67, 79, 87, 113, 114, 124, 142, 143, 230
Goal Orientation 108
Good Decision................... See Leadership: Making Good Decision
Guinier 128, 230
Guo 51, 229

H

Hall.....89, 124, 230, 236, 239
Halloran 44, 125, 127, 129, 131, 230
Hands-Off......................... 129
Hawthorn Experiment 102
Herzberg..................... 88, 230
Hou............................53, 230
House 38, 124, 204, 205, 231, 236
Huang 196, 227, 231, 241, 242

Hughes 160, 231, 233, 237
Human Resource Management 121

I

Ideal-Type 26, 106, 107
Ideal-Type Characteristics of Management Behaviors 106
Inducement of Reward.... 168, 191
Influence . 28, 58, 59, 60, 144, 145, 146, 148, 151, 152, 153, 155, 156, 158, 159, 160, 163, 164, 168, 169, 170, 171, 176, 192, 193, 194, 195, 197, 199, 200, 212, 219, 220, 221, 222, 223
Influencing.....58, 59, 60, 152, 153, 156, 190, 197
Influential Outcome 143
Information Technology ...121
Instrumental goals........... 109
Intended Audience xvi
Internal (Organizational) Environment................ 187
Interpersonal influence 58
Isonen...................... 182, 231
Ivancevich 69, 230, 231

J

Jill Annis xi
John Dewey.......................181
Justice ....See Kindness and Justice

K

Kahn .. 156, 158, 190, 194, 232
Karakitapoglu-Aygün ...51, 55, 232

Katie Hayne xi
Katz 156, 158, 190, 191, 194, 232
Kelloway 131, 232
Kindness .... See Kindness and Justice
Kindness and Justice 96
Koontz........................ 72, 232
Koveshnikov 51, 168, 232
Krishali 64, 67, 74, 232

L

Laissez-fair 129
Laissez-Fair Management Technique......................129
Landmine Dilemma of Leadership.....................214
Lara Tewksbury....................xi
Laura Vosika...................... xiii
Lawler 115, 226
Lawrence Diggs xii
Leader does the right thing 173
Leader walks the talk 174
Leaders conquer the context 172
Leaders Do the Right Thing! 141
Leaders Eat Last....... 210, 238
Leaders Protect their Followers 207
Leadershipxvii, xix, 41, 45, 57, 143, 147, 148, 152, 164, 176, 192, 197, 198, 201, 209, 212, 219, 221, 225, 226, 227, 228, 229, 230, 231, 232, 233, 234, 236, 237, 238, 239, 240, 241, 242, 252
Charisma 160

Doing the Right Thing .. 172
Ethos............................ 161
Factors that Affect Doing the Right Thing 175
Followership.................. 161
Goal Attainment............ 152
Good Political Skills......212
Human Relations Techniques 198
Influence Through Endorsed Power........ 155
Informal Status 145
inspirational appeal 155
Logos 161
Making Good Decisions 176
Pathos 160
Perceptions and Relativity of Managerial Authority 169
Provision of Protection 207
rational persuasion 156
Vision Orientation 200
Voluntary Extraordinary Performance..............194
Leadership Competencies. 145
Leadership Factor 219
Leadership Is Influence 142
LEADERSHIP IS INFLUENCE 142
Leadership Misnomers 41
Leading 36, 37, 39, 40, 41, 42, 64, 68, 69, 128, 217, 252
Lee............................ 54, 233
Leymann 131, 233
Li 50, 51, 228, 233, 234, 242
Lincoln Adult Soccer Association League 165
Lippitt 52, 53, 241
Logos.. See Leadership: Logos
Lowe...................28, 233, 240
Lussier .. 54, 59, 190, 196, 233

M

Mackenzie Reuss................. xi
Maintenance of Zone of
Indifference.................. 136
Management 55, 56, 72, 75,
76, 99, 109, 119, 120, 121,
122, 125, 129, 132, 149, 180,
219, 225, 226, 227, 228,
229, 231, 232, 233, 234,
235, 236, 237, 238, 239,
240, 241, 242
Management Basics..150, 234
Management Factor 216
Management Techniques .119,
120, 226
Management Training.....180,
See Leadership:
Management Training
Manager Hurts Members ..211
Managers Do Things Right
.... 105
Manager-Subordinate
Relations 112
Marketing Management....121
Material Order 95
Max Weber .....See Weber, See
Weber
Mayo..........................102, 234
McClelland 205, 234
McCormack............... 161, 234
Meindl 159, 234
Meng..........................53, 234
Merriam-Webster Dictionary
......................................235
Merton......... 42, 181, 182, 235
Metz.........................38, 235
Meyer..............................235
Miller.................130, 131, 235
Minority Leader 38
misnomers......................... 41

Mitchell 204, 231
Mshvenieradze...........161, 235

N

Nanus ...57, 134, 173, 190, 227
National Party of Nigeria—
NPN...............................38
Nigeria...37, 38, 185, 225, 235
Non-coercive influence 58, 59,
158, 162, 219

O

Obedient Compliance by
Subordinates................. 117
Occupational Psychosis.....181
O'Donnell 72, 232
Ofstad 174, 235
Ondo State 38, 236
Ondo State House of
Assembly........................38
Operations Management...121
Ordering Function 68
Organizational Bureaucracy
.108, 114, 116, 117, 122, 134,
183, 184, 199
Organizational Citizenship
Behaviors 123
Organizational Culture..... 187
Organizational Dysfunctional
Behaviors 131
Organizational Effectiveness
and Efficiency 121
Organizational Environments
.... 185, 186
Organizational Structure...42,
47, 72, 91, 92, 93, 94, 95,
113, 114, 115, 118, 133, 146,
176, 191, 220
Organizational Systems... 135,
136

Organizations Determine Managers 61
Organizing 66
Overview and Takeaways .. 215
Oyinlade vi, xix, 154, 156, 236, 251

P

Parsons 109, 110, 236
Participative Management 124, 125, 126, 127
Participative Management Technique 125
Path-Goal Theory 124, 205, 231
PathosSee Leadership: Pathos
Pellegrini 49, 236
Peng 53, 230
Perackovic 76, 236
Peters 27, 44, 45, 236
Pizzolitto 196, 237
Planning and Forecasting .. 65
Positive Outcomes of Rulership 52
Postema 117, 237
Practical Judgement .... See Leadership: Making Good Decisions
Preface xvii
Prescriptive Management Functions 63
Pride 59, 154, 190, 237
Principle of Authority and Responsibility 79
Principle of Discipline 80
Principle of Division of Work 75
Principle of Equity 96
Principle of Esprit De Corps 102

Principle of Initiative 101
Principle of Order 94
Principle of Remuneration 88
Principle of Stability of Tenure 99
Principle of the Scalar Chain 91
Principle of Unity of Command 83
Principle of Unity of Direction 84
Principles of Management .. 74
Professional Deformation 181, 231
Proscriptive Management Functions 63
Purwanto 49, 123, 237

R

Rahmani 54, 237
Raison D'etre 26
Ralph. C. Davis .... See Davis
Rational and legal 42
Rational Decisions 186
Rational-legal 42
Ratliff 177, 178, 237
Reciprocal Relationship 163
Related Concepts in Headship 47
Revisiting Headeship 216
Ridgeway 52, 53, 237
Robert Merton ...... See Merton
Rodrigues 153, 237
Rulership .. xix, 31, 48, 49, 50, 51, 52, 53, 56, 57, 59, 122

S

Sagie 55, 238
Sanchez-Manzanares . 53, 238
Scandura 49, 232, 236

Schaubroeck........ 51, 123, 238
Scott xiv, xv, 114, 117, 157, 228
Scott Powers...................... xiv
Second Republic 37
Sentimental Decisions 185
Sevel 117, 238
Sherry Helmke xiii
Simon 136, 192, 210, 238
Sinek...........................210, 238
Sladjana......................195, 238
Smith 76, 239
Social Order 95
Social Structures and Social
   Theories...........................181
Staffing 64, 71
Staffing and Coordinating ...71
Stalker 94, 227
Star City Rangers 165
Steers...........................29, 239
Stein.....................45, 56, 239
Stogdill 57, 226, 239
suffocating conditions 173,
   180
Suffocating contexts 173

T

Tannenbaum 58, 239
Taylor 64, 76, 78, 239
Technical Judgment .... See
   Leadership: Making Good
   Decisions
Terry 69, 239
The Protestant Ethic and the
   Spirit of Capitalism. 76, 241
The Tyranny of the Majority
  128
Threat of Punishment...... 156,
   162, 168, 171, 191, 221
Tolbert 89, 124, 239
Tom Shirazi xi

U

Uhl-Bien 168, 240
Understanding Leadership141
Understanding Management
   61
Unity Party of Nigeria 38

V

Value judgment................ 178
Vasilescu......28, 144, 221, 240
Veblen...............180, 213, 240
Vinegar Museum xii
Voluntary compliance 58, 195,
   196
Vroom......................204, 240

W

Wang ..54, 227, 231, 233, 234,
   240
Watson 114, 240
Weber 42, 76, 106, 114, 133,
   156, 240, 241
What is Leadership? 57
What is Management?........ 55
What is Ruling? 48
What We Need Now Are
   Leaders............................ 27
White 52, 53, 241
Wolinski 60, 197, 241
Wood 136, 241
World Bank Data 28, 241
Wu 51, 241, 242

X

Xie.............................51, 242

Y

Yao 51, 242

Yukl 156, 242

Yun 49, 242

Z

Zachary Christo ....See Christo

Zhang 51, 231, 233, 242

Zone of Acceptance .. 136, 190, 192, 193, 221

Zone of Indifference..115, 136, 138, 139, 190, 191, 192, 193, 194, 221, 222

ABOUT THE AUTHOR

A. Olu Oyinlade, PhD., is a Leadership Specialist and Consultant. He is a Business Organizational Sociologist and Professor in the Department of Sociology and Anthropology at the University of Nebraska, Omaha. He is also the President and Principal Consultant of Crown Business Consulting, LLC, in Omaha, which specializes in *leadership development consulting*. He has published many scientific research articles on organizational leadership, one of which is his invented standards-based method of measuring leadership effectiveness named the *Essential Behavioral Leadership Qualities* (EBLQ) method. Since the EBLQ was published in Performance Improvement Quarterly (a leading academic journal for performance improvement) in 2008, it has been widely read across the world and used by many leadership scholars and consultants. Professor Oyinlade is a Nigerian-born American who infuses his international and cross-cultural background with his scientific knowledge of organizational science to develop a rich understanding of organizational leadership and technical human relations competencies for helping managers become leaders.

The content of this book represents only the intellectual product of the author. It does not represent the opinions of any other organization or entity.